Sustainability and youth work

Editor
Ellie Keen

Authors
Ellie Keen
Justina Pinkeviciute
Alan Hayes
Agi Berecz
Burcu Meltem Arık Akyüz

Council of Europe

Illustrations: Matia Losego
Cover photos: Shutterstock.com
Layout and cover design:
Documents and Publications Production
Department (SPDP), Council of Europe

Council of Europe Publishing
F-67075 Strasbourg Cedex
http://book.coe.int

ISBN 978-92-871-8578-5
© Council of Europe and European Commission,
June 2018
Printed at the Council of Europe

Welcome to the T-Kit series

Some of you may have wondered: what does T-Kit mean? We can offer at least two answers. The first is as simple as the full version in English: "training kit". The second has more to do with the sound of "T-Kit", the word that may easily recall "ticket", one of the travel documents we usually need to go on a journey. For us, this T-Kit is a tool that each of us can use in our work.

More specifically, we would like to address youth workers and trainers, and offer them theoretical and practical tools to work with and use when training young people.

The T-Kit Series is the result of a collective effort involving people from different cultural, professional and organisational backgrounds. Youth trainers, youth leaders in NGOs and professional writers have worked together in order to create high-quality publications that address the needs of the target group while recognising the diversity of approaches across Europe to each subject.

The T-Kits are a product of the partnership between the European Commission and the Council of Europe in the field of youth.

To find out more, visit the website:
pjp-eu.coe.int/en/web/youth-partnership

Contents

CHAPTER 1 – INTRODUCTION   **5**

CHAPTER 2 – SUSTAINABILITY: THE ISSUES   7

    What is sustainability?   7

    Sustainable Development Goals   8

    Europe and sustainability   9

CHAPTER 3 – EDUCATION AND YOUTH WORK FOR SUSTAINABILITY   **15**

    Education for sustainability   15

    Youth work for sustainability   15

    Aims and objectives of education for sustainability   16

    Knowledge, skills and attitudes   17

    Methodological principles   18

    Using the activities   21

CHAPTER 4 – ACTIVITIES   **23**

    Summary of activities   24

CHAPTER 5 – MAKING A DIFFERENCE   105

    The importance of hope   105

    Picking your issue   106

    Campaigning and advocacy   109

    Planning an action   110

CHAPTER 6 – SUSTAINABILITY CHECKLIST   **113**

    Management and working practices   113

    Management of office and youth space   114

    Meetings and gatherings   115

BIBLIOGRAPHY   117

Chapter 1
Introduction

Human beings are responsible for a number of crises which threaten the very future of life on earth. For centuries, we have treated the planet as if its natural resources were limitless and as if we could spoil them, use them and then discard them. We have spilt billions of litres of oil into the seas, cleared millions of acres of rainforest, mined deep underground, producing toxic slag heaps, stripped the natural minerals from the soil through industrial farming methods, and filled the atmosphere with dangerous levels of carbon dioxide, leading to potential climate breakdown. The list could be continued, but the last item alone could put an end to all life on earth.

However, there is now a growing realisation that such profligate practices are not only harmful for other living creatures on the planet, they are also potentially fatal for humans. In developing countries, in particular, the results are already being seen: droughts, hurricanes and other natural disasters are destroying people's homes and livelihoods and are also a major factor in the flood of refugees seeking a better life. Many of these refugees are ending up in Europe, making it more difficult for our politicians to avert their gaze from problems in less developed countries. Europe has perhaps contributed more than any other region to these problems. Now we need to recognise our role in causing them, and play an active part in trying to resolve them.

Education is one means of doing so. It is the next generations who will increasingly see the consequences of climate change – and other problems – and the consequences will not be confined to the less developed regions. Already Europe has seen increasingly erratic and extreme weather events, and these will increase in future years. So young people need to understand and take the lead both in adopting more sustainable lifestyles and in creating solutions for the region as a whole.

This manual is a practical tool to begin that process. It is designed primarily for youth workers and educators to introduce the topic of sustainability to young people in a non-formal setting. However, it will also be suitable for groups of youth workers, youth leaders or educators who may be looking for training on the topic of sustainability. By means of the activities in the main body of the manual, young people and those who work with them can familiarise themselves with some of the problems facing the globe, and begin to discuss solutions. The last two chapters of the manual take matters further: this is an opportunity for youth groups to begin to make a difference in their locality, and perhaps beyond.

CHAPTER OUTLINE

Chapter 2. Sustainability: the issues

Chapter 2 looks at the definition of "sustainability" and "sustainable development" and describes the international efforts to put sustainability on the agenda of national governments, in particular through the Sustainable Development Goals (SDGs). The last section of the chapter explores Europe's record on sustainability.

Chapter 3. Education and youth work for sustainability

Chapter 3 introduces the idea of education for sustainability and includes some practical and methodological advice for running the activities in Chapter 4.

Chapter 4. Activities

Chapter 4 includes 18 activities on sustainability, at different levels of complexity and addressing a number of different issues. Each activity contains detailed instructions, and some also provide additional background information. The last part of each activity makes some suggestions for how young people can take forward the work done in the session and begin to make a difference in their communities.

Chapter 5. Making a difference

Chapter 5 will help you with supporting your group to take action in the community: it offers some background principles and methodological advice, including on planning actions with a group. It also contains a number of examples of groups "making a difference", which you can use as inspiration.

Chapter 6. Sustainability checklist

Chapter 6 contains a number of ideas which the group could implement, for example in the youth centre, in the locality, or even at international meetings.

Chapter 2
Sustainability: the issues

This chapter addresses some of the central concepts, concerns and initiatives related to sustainable development:

- ▶ in Section 1, we look at the definition and evolution of the terms "sustainable" and "sustainability";
- ▶ in Section 2, we outline the United Nations' drive to put sustainability on the agenda of national governments, in particular through the Sustainable Development Goals (SDGs);
- ▶ section 3 explores Europe's record on sustainability, and successes and failures in contributing to the future sustainability of the planet.

WHAT IS SUSTAINABILITY?

Perhaps we should begin with what it means to be "sustainable". The dictionary defines this as being "able to be maintained at a certain rate or level" (Oxford Dictionaries, https://en.oxforddictionaries.com. Clearly the current pace of human activity cannot be "maintained" at the same level: carbon emissions are leading to climate breakdown, industrial farming methods and the demand for minerals and raw materials are leading to depletion of the earth's resources, to degradation of the soil, to pollution of air, sea and water, to mass extinctions among the animal and insect worlds – among numerous other problems.

The earth cannot tolerate this, nor can humanity. In this sense, our current habits are not sustainable.

This consideration, which has become increasingly evident in recent years, has led to a secondary dictionary meaning for the word "sustainable": "conserving an ecological balance by avoiding depletion of natural resources" (Oxford Dictionaries, https://en.oxforddictionaries.com. Among "natural resources" are included not only those we can see, hear or touch – such as oil and gas, gold, diamonds and uranium – but also less tangible resources, such as the pH value of the sea, and therefore its ability to support the life of certain marine organisms; the amount of carbon dioxide in the atmosphere, which regulates the temperature of the planet; the fertility of the soil, and so on.

Sustainability is the state of being sustainable. It is the state where human beings and the natural world exist in harmony, without destroying each other (and themselves).

"Sustainable development" is the process of moving towards sustainability. Sustainable development aims to improve the quality of life of human beings, including future generations, by reconciling economic growth, social development and environmental protection.

> "[Sustainable development is] development that meets the needs of the present without compromising the ability of future generations to meet their own needs." (United Nations 1992)

More than being "green"...

Sustainability is not only about addressing environmental threats, it is also about ensuring that everyone is able to enjoy the full set of human rights, in a way which does not jeopardise the rights of human beings in the future. These rights should include social and economic, civil and political, cultural and environmental rights. In other words, sustainability demands a quality of life for all which not only meets physical needs, but also meets social and cultural needs, and which is distributed equitably.

For this reason, it is now accepted that sustainable development demands action across at least three different dimensions: environmental protection, social inclusion and economic development. The relation between these three dimensions can be illustrated by the Venn diagram in Figure 1: actions in the economic realm must satisfy the needs of social inclusion, and our social demands must satisfy environmental possibilities.

Figure 1. Dimensions of sustainable development

A sustainable world is one where economic growth and social inclusion are contained within the environmental limits that will allow the model to continue into the future:

- ▶ the dimension of environmental protection includes questions relating to stewardship of the planet's natural resources, e.g. water, air, minerals, carbon deposits, flora and fauna. This dimension also includes the impact on the environment of housing, agriculture, emissions and waste, etc.;
- ▶ the social dimension refers to issues such as equality, democracy, human rights, social justice, community resilience and adaptation to environmental challenges;
- ▶ the economic dimension refers to practices associated with production, the use and management of resources, and also to issues such as consumption, technology, labour and wealth distribution.

A fourth dimension is sometimes added to these three, that of cultural sustainability. The cultural dimension relates to cultural identity, diversity, creativity, the role of art, memory, heritage, spirituality and community planning.

"Sustainable human development will occur when all humans can have fulfilling lives without degrading the planet." (Global Footprint Network 2003)

SUSTAINABLE DEVELOPMENT GOALS

In 2015, to build on the success of the Millennium Development Goals, the member states of the United Nations adopted a set of 17 new goals, known as the Sustainable Development Goals (SDGs, see Figure 2). The programme incorporating these goals is known as the 2030 Agenda for Sustainable Development, as the goals are meant to be achieved by 2030. Unlike the Millennium Development Goals, the SDGs apply not only to developing nations, but to all nations around the world.

Figure 2. Sustainable Development Goals

Source: United Nations

The overall aims of Agenda 2030 are to put an end to poverty, protect the planet and ensure prosperity for all. In this way, the SDGs reflect current thinking about the three (or four) dimensions of sustainability. A brief glance at the range of goals and the issues to be addressed confirms the broad notion of sustainability which has been adopted, extending far beyond mere environmental protection.

Each of the goals contains a number of specific targets to be achieved by 2030. For example:

Goal 7: Affordable and Clean Energy includes the following targets, among others:

- ▸ to ensure universal access to affordable, reliable and modern energy services;
- ▸ to increase substantially the share of renewable energy in the global energy mix;
- ▸ to double the global rate of improvement in energy efficiency;

Goal 4: Quality Education includes the following targets, among others:

- ▸ to ensure that all girls and boys complete free, equitable and quality primary and secondary education;
- ▸ to ensure equal access for all women and men to affordable and quality technical, vocational and tertiary education, including university;
- ▸ to substantially increase the number of youth and adults who have relevant skills, including technical and vocational skills, for employment, decent jobs and entrepreneurship;
- ▸ to ensure that all learners acquire the knowledge and skills needed to promote sustainable development, including, among others, through education for sustainable development and sustainable lifestyles, human rights, gender equality, promotion of a culture of peace and non-violence, global citizenship and appreciation of cultural diversity and of culture's contribution to sustainable development.

Further information can be found at www.un.org/sustainabledevelopment.

EUROPE AND SUSTAINABILITY

Europe has mixed results when it comes to sustainability. In many respects, it is among the worst regions of the world, both in terms of the damage it is causing to the planet and human existence today, and in terms of historical damage caused. However, a few positive improvements have been observed in recent years across the region as a whole. Of course, the results in different countries across the region display considerable diversity.

Europe's ecological deficit

An "ecological footprint" is a measure of the area of biologically productive land and water an individual, population or activity requires to produce all the resources it consumes and to sequester its waste.

"Biocapacity" or "Biological capacity" represents a region's biologically productive land and sea area available to provide ecosystem services for human use. These services include providing food and timber, hosting human infrastructure, and absorbing waste such as carbon dioxide emissions from fossil fuel.

An "ecological deficit" or "reserve" is the difference between the ecological footprint and the biocapacity of a region or country. An ecological deficit occurs when the footprint of a population exceeds the biocapacity of the area available to that population. An ecological reserve occurs when the available biocapacity of an area exceeds the footprint of that area's population.

(Global Footprint Network, www.footprintnetwork.org/resources/glossary/, accessed 21 February 2018)

Europe's ecological footprint has seen rapid growth and now greatly exceeds the region's biocapacity. For the 28 states of the European Union (EU) and the 33 states of the European Economic Area, the ecological footprint is almost three times the size of the corresponding region's biocapacity. This means that if everyone on the planet had the same ecological footprint as the average resident of either of these areas, nearly three earths would be needed to support the demands on nature.

Figure 3 shows that Europe's lifestyle demands have become increasingly problematic and unsustainable, rising from an average footprint of just over one "earth" in the 1960s to an average of nearly three "earths" today.

As a comparison, Figure 4 shows the ecological footprints in "number of earths" for Europe, for the world as a whole, and for Africa. Africa, as can be seen, still has an average ecological footprint which does not exceed one "earth".

Figure 5 illustrates the variation across the globe in ecological deficits or reserves. The red shaded areas represent countries in deficit, and those shaded green represent countries whose ecological footprint is smaller than the biocapacity of the country. It can be seen that even within Europe, there is wide variation in the demands which different countries are making on the earth's resources. It should be noted that these demands are a function not only of the way the population lives, but also of the size of the population relative to the country area concerned. Russia, for example, shows up as a "biocapacity creditor" mainly because the area of land it covers is so immense and its population is relatively sparse.

Figure 3. Historical increase in ecological deficit (Europe)

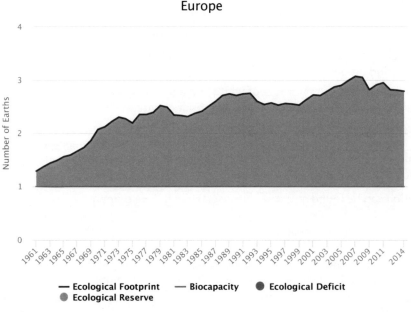

Source: Global Footprint Network (2017)

Figure 4. Ecological footprint comparison (2013)

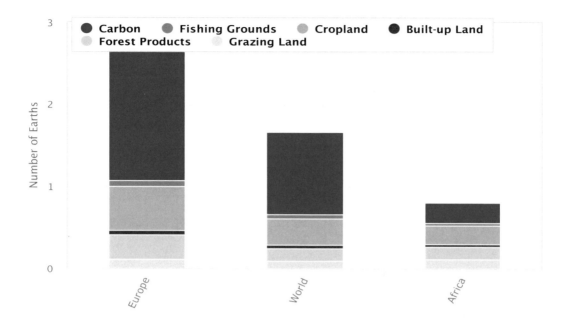

Source: Global Footprint Network (2017), 2017 National Footprint Accounts

Figure 5. Countries in ecological deficit/reserve

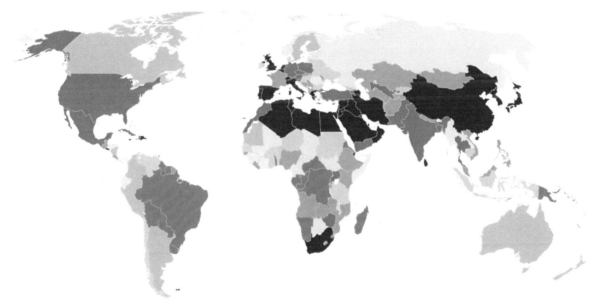

ECOLOGICAL DEFICIT/RESERVE

An ecological deficit occurs when the ecological footprint of a population exceeds the biocapacity of the area available to that population. A national ecological deficit means that the nation is importing biocapacity through trade, liquidating national ecological assets or emitting carbon dioxide waste into the atmosphere. An ecological reserve exists when the biocapacity of a region exceeds its population's ecological footprint.

Source: Global Footprint Network (2017)

Carbon emissions

Figure 4 also tells us that the largest single component of overshoot in Europe when it comes to sustainability is our consumption of carbon. In fact, the EU is the third biggest emitter of carbon dioxide in the world, after China and the United States, and these three regions together contribute more than half of total global emissions (Figure 6). The bottom 100 countries only account for 3.5%.

If per capita emissions are considered, Europe's ranking improves, but it still manages to emit twice as much as Asia, and almost eight times more than Africa.

However, today's emissions are only part of the story. Europe's industry and resource-heavy lifestyle has in fact done far more damage to the planet than its position in today's rankings might suggest. Europe was the birthplace of modern industry, and the historical emissions produced by countries in this region are responsible for a large proportion of the greenhouse gases currently accumulated in the atmosphere. These historical accumulations lie behind the unsustainable levels of CO_2 in the atmosphere, and are therefore partly, if not mainly responsible for today's crisis. Many developing nations see it as unfair that in international negotiations about carbon emissions they are required to make similar sacrifices to developed nations, although their contribution to the problem has been negligible. Furthermore, it was industrialisation fuelled by sources of carbon such as oil and coal which allowed the richer nations to achieve the levels of economic development that raised standards of living and levels of health and well-being for their populations. Developing nations, which are more likely to suffer from the effects of climate change, justifiably feel that their world has been spoiled, but not by them.

Figure 6. Carbon dioxide emissions for the top 40 countries by emissions in 2013 (totals and per capita, GT – giga tonnes, T/p – tonnes/capita)

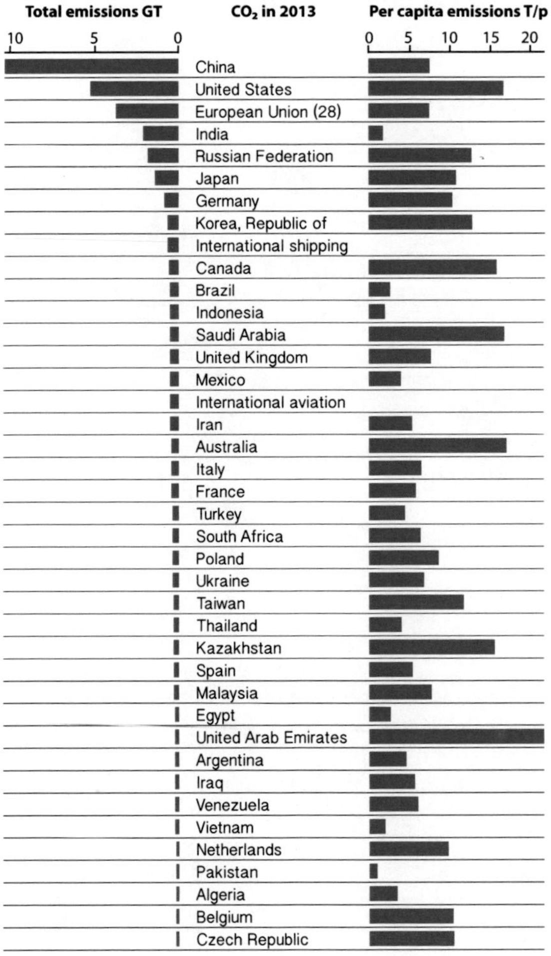

Data from EU Edgar database
Source: Wikimedia, available at https://bit.ly/2ATsLoq, accessed 10 February 2018

The EU Emissions Trading System (EU ETS)

EU ETS was established in 2005 to allow industry to buy and sell "emission allowances", with the aim of reducing overall carbon emissions. In 2010, the European Commission claimed that the scheme had led to reductions of more than 8% (European Commission 2011). However, environmental groups have disputed this and have been heavily critical of a scheme which is solely market-based and susceptible to fraud and gaming (Corporate Europe Observatory 2015). It also appears likely that much of the reduction in emissions which has been achieved in recent years is a result of an increasing share of energy being provided by renewable sources in Europe. This, at least, is a very positive development but it is mostly a consequence of other factors, rather than the ETS.

The role of business

Europe's approach, and in particular the EU's approach towards improving sustainability, has often been market oriented and has given priority to corporate interests. For example, human rights groups have criticised the EU for the lack of coherence between its trade practice and its pledge to eradicate global poverty. The Common Agricultural Policy has an adverse impact on food sovereignty, while access to affordable and life-saving medicines in developing countries is undermined by Europe's trade agreements.

For some, the planetary ecological crisis has created opportunities to make money. Fresh water scarcity, for example, has often been used as an opening for privatisation and investment, and banks have increasingly tried to buy up water rights in strategic areas around the world. Profits can be made by increasing the price of water and making it inaccessible for the most vulnerable people.

To add insult to injury, the privatisation of water and other natural resources is defended on the grounds that it offers the best way of protecting a scarce resource. Those profiting from the policy proudly display their "sustainability certificates", and turn up at international conferences for water conservation.

Other companies have been known to create sustainable arms of their industry to mask – or greenwash – some of the damage done by their primary business. For example, oil companies – some of the biggest contributors to climate change – are now entering the renewable energy market, and often publicise this to draw attention away from other more polluting activities. Chemical companies, with long records of toxic pollution, are moving into the water and air purification businesses while continuing to pollute with the rest of their industrial output. Companies can even profit from their own polluting activities, by bidding to clean it up and earning social credit in addition to making a financial profit. Young people need to learn to look beyond the headlines, and beyond corporate marketing, to see the real impact on the globe of commercial practices – and often, the real impact of their own consumption.

Positive initiatives

There are of course numerous inspiring initiatives which aim to address the challenges to sustainability. These initiatives range from the individual or local to changes in legislation or political initiatives, at national, regional or even international level. Some examples of grass-roots initiatives are provided in Chapter 5, "Making a difference", including a number of activities in which young people could become involved. The examples below have been taken from regional or international level, but it should be noted that when change happens at the political level, this has nearly always been preceded by continuous campaigning and lobbying, often involving thousands or tens of thousands of individuals and organisations working together over a period of many years.

Cutting e-waste

The European Commission reached an agreement with major phone manufacturers to produce the same type of charger for all mobile phones sold in the EU. One of the reasons for this initiative was to cut the amount of electronic waste, so that a new charger would not be needed every time a new phone was bought. It is estimated that discarded phone chargers produce 51 000 tonnes of e-waste per year in the EU. This voluntary agreement to reduce unnecessary production has been followed by a binding resolution obliging all manufacturers to provide a common battery charger.

Cycling in Europe

The Copenhagenize Index records the "best" cities for urban cycling according to 14 parameters. In 2017, 18 of the 20 most cycle-friendly cities in the world were in Europe. An increasing number of people are choosing cycling as their preferred way to commute and a cycling culture has become mainstream in numerous countries. Many environmentally and socially motivated cyclists are trying to transform our cities from being car-centric to becoming bicycle and pedestrian friendly. Governments and local governments are following or sometimes leading the trend by investing in cycle share schemes and creating cycle lanes.

The Aarhus Convention

When it comes to the right to participate in decision making, the most important instrument in environmental matters is the Aarhus Convention. This treaty has been ratified by the great majority of European states and by the EU. It has been hugely influential in granting the public the right to receive environmental information, participate in environmental decision making and challenge public decisions when these fail to respect environmental law.

The Basel Ban

The Basel Convention was adopted in 1989 and was designed to control the disposal of hazardous waste. However, many countries and organisations felt it did not go far enough, and campaigned for a total ban on sending hazardous waste to less developed countries. In 1995, such a ban was included in an amendment to the Basel Convention. It was known as the Basel Ban. This amendment has been accepted by 86 countries and by the EU, and will enter into force when agreed to by three quarters of the member states to the Basel Convention.

Chapter 3
Education and youth work for sustainability

This chapter introduces the idea of education for sustainability and includes some practical and methodological advice for running the activities in Chapter 4.

EDUCATION FOR SUSTAINABILITY

> Education for Sustainable Development (ESD) is about shaping a better tomorrow for all – and it must start today. (UNESCO 2014)

In December 2002, the UN General Assembly declared the Decade of Education for Sustainable Development (2005-2014). The United Nations Educational, Scientific and Cultural Organization (UNESCO) was appointed as lead agency for the promotion of this initiative, and when it came to an end it introduced a new Global Action Programme (GAP) on Education for Sustainable Development.

The purpose of GAP is "to generate and scale up action in all levels and areas of education and learning to accelerate progress towards sustainable development" (UNESCO 2014). It has two objectives:

- ► "to reorient education and learning so that everyone has the opportunity to acquire the knowledge, skills, values and attitudes that empower them to contribute to sustainable development;
- ► to strengthen education and learning in all agendas, programmes and activities that promote sustainable development." (UNESCO 2014)

YOUTH WORK FOR SUSTAINABILITY

One of the core ideas of sustainability is that each generation inherits the earth from those who have come before them. The aim of every generation should be to leave it in better, or at least in no worse, condition than when it found it. Youth work can play an important role in ensuring that this happens: in addition to the family and the formal education system, youth work exerts a strong influence on young people's transition to adulthood, and it can help in promoting their participation in society.

Youth work has a long tradition of supporting young people's understanding of the world around them and promoting such values as justice and equality.

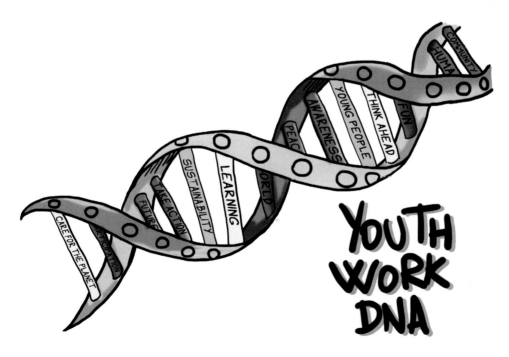

The DNA of youth work

There is no internationally agreed definition of youth work or its outcomes, and there are various methods and models of youth work. Some of these include:

- ▸ recreational;
- ▸ personal development;
- ▸ critical social education;
- ▸ radical social change.

Youth workers often engage young people with issues such as citizenship, interdependence, diversity, intercultural dialogue and learning, social issues and sustainability, all with a view to affecting the knowledge, skills, values and attitudes which govern how people interact with the world around them. These issues are all closely related to sustainability, and anyone working to explore them with young people is already engaging in education for sustainability!

Youth work for sustainability uses many of the issues raised in Chapter 2 to explore the topic in an interactive and non-formal way, including by providing opportunities for young people to participate and even to direct the learning process themselves. The aim of youth work for sustainability is not just for young people to find out about sustainability, but for them to begin to appreciate its importance and engage in promoting it.

Such work can take a practical approach to understanding sustainability issues, and can offer a wide range of options for taking this knowledge forward and "making a difference" – as outlined in Chapter 5. Education for sustainability in a non-formal setting can open up possibilities for young people to learn about and take part in existing local and global movements, and can help them develop their own skills and desire for a more sustainable lifestyle.

Youth work for sustainability can therefore mean a number of different things. The following list offers a few suggestions for ways to engage young people in sustainability and support their learning:

- ▸ sessions, workshops, project visits, group discussions or other educational activities with a sustainability focus, designed to influence young people's attitudes to sustainability;
- ▸ projects addressing sustainability issues, initiated by a group of young people and supported by youth workers;
- ▸ opportunities for young people to become involved in sustainability campaigns at a local level, perhaps with other members of the local community;
- ▸ improving the sustainability of the youth centre, e.g. by addressing waste or energy use, setting up a repair café, or using land around the centre to grow vegetables;
- ▸ international non-formal exchanges or learning projects in which one or a group of young people take part and learn about sustainability issues (e.g. local or international volunteering projects, youth gatherings, international youth exchanges);
- ▸ encouraging young people to challenge assumptions and actions that are detrimental to an inclusive and equal society, e.g. through local research, conducting interviews, or lobbying or campaigning against unsustainable practices either locally or at national or international level;
- ▸ altering personal habits to become more sustainable or working as a group to increase the sustainability of the youth centre.

AIMS AND OBJECTIVES OF EDUCATION FOR SUSTAINABILITY

To create a world that is more just, peaceful and sustainable, all individuals and societies must be equipped and empowered by knowledge, skills and values as well as be instilled with a heightened awareness to drive such change. This is where education has a critical role to play. (UNESCO 2014)

The activities in this manual are designed to support the general aims and objectives of youth work for sustainability. In particular, they are intended to:

- ▸ develop young people's knowledge of environmental and social issues at local and global level, for example with regard to:

- whether fish sold in the local supermarket have been caught in a way that is likely to endanger future populations (see the activity "Fishing game");
- where plastic wrapping is likely to end up (see "Waste manifesto");
- what the impact of our own habits may be on children in other parts of the world (see "Take a step forward");

▶ promote understanding of key concepts and principles related to sustainability, for example:
- carbon emissions (see "Chain reaction" or "Climate superhero auditions");
- sustainable agriculture (see "Chicken sandwich");
- pollution (see "The cost of fashion" or "Waste manifesto");

▶ develop critical thinking skills and encourage participants to question prevailing opinions, where necessary, for example:
- the activity "Greenwashing" encourages participants to look beyond advertising claims made by companies;
- "A finite planet" is a discussion activity which looks at some commonly held views about common priorities for the economy;

▶ encourage active participation in order to promote sustainability, including at the personal, local or global scale:
- see Chapter 5, "Making a difference", in particular, but each of the activities contains ideas for action at the end;

▶ strengthen values relevant to sustainability, for example: empathy, equality, solidarity, responsibility, concern for future generations, appreciation of nature;
- all of the activities aim to promote values by giving young people the space to discuss and question what they regard as important. The starter activity "Needs and wants" can be used to spark discussion on what is really important – both to participants individually, and to the planet.

KNOWLEDGE, SKILLS AND ATTITUDES

Learning for sustainability is a process involving the cognitive, affective and psychomotor dimensions. This means that we need to involve participants in a transformative process as individuals, by engaging each of these three elements. We can think of this as involving Head (thinking), Heart (feeling) and Hands (doing). Uniting these three domains helps young people acquire the knowledge, skills and attitudes that are needed to build a more sustainable, peaceful and just world. Figure 7 indicates the type of questions that might be raised to engage the head, heart and hands.

Example:

Learning about sustainable food production can be approached by learning the principles of organic gardening (Head), sharing our personal motivations for being interested in alternative food production (Heart), and getting one's hands dirty by sowing seeds and harvesting homegrown organic vegetables (Hands).

To shift participants' learning from the personal to the local level, we could try activities such as the following:

▶ introduce them to the local shopping community or community-supported agricultural system, if one exists;
▶ organise a local market day;
▶ offer help to the local school to help it cultivate a garden.

To move the project to the global level, we could encourage activities such as the following:

▶ join solidarity campaigns to support small farmers around the world fighting against large corporations;
▶ join a protest against the privatisation of seeds;
▶ protest such privatisation by organising a community seed swap project, or starting a local seed bank.

This T-Kit strives to ensure harmony between different learning objectives, and all of the educational activities involve a balance between knowledge (Head), values and attitudes (Heart) and skills (Hands).

Figure 7. Head, heart and hands as learning objectives

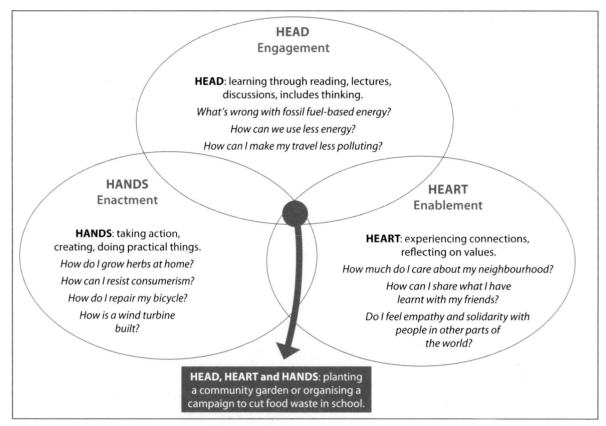

Source: adapted from Sipos, Battisti and Grimm (2008)

METHODOLOGICAL PRINCIPLES

Vision without action is a dream. Action without vision is a waste of time. Vision with action can change the world. *(Nelson Mandela)*

This section contains practical advice on running the activities contained in Chapter 4.

Group working methods

When working on sustainability, it is important that the way a group works and learns together reflects the values and the change that the learning is supposed to bring about. A group needs to be cohesive and act as a whole, while also maintaining respect for the uniqueness of each individual and for the range of opinions within the group.

The main role of a youth worker or educator is to facilitate the activity or discussion: to ease the exchange of views, thoughts and feelings within the group of young people. As facilitators, it is important to make sure that everyone takes part, everyone is heard, and that the conversation is fluid and interesting. The facilitator aims to hold the space for the group while fading into the background.

Theme-centred interaction

The Swiss psychologist Ruth Cohn described four different elements within a group learning process:

- ▶ I (the individual): the motivations, interests, personal histories and levels of involvement of individual participants, as well as the "luggage" they may bring with them;
- ▶ We (the group): the relationships, dynamics and types of co-operation within the group;
- ▶ It (the topic): the subjects and content of the training;
- ▶ Globe: the training and organisational environment (also partly represented by the participants) (The Ruth Cohn Institution for TCI – International).

This is a useful classification because it helps us to see that most group gatherings tend to focus on the third level – the subject and content of the session. Particularly in formal education, this is generally believed to be the most important element of learning. However, this often results in the "I" and "We" remaining hidden. Unresolved issues at these levels may then distract the group learning process. For example, participants may ask themselves questions such as:

- ▶ am I accepted by the group?
- ▶ does my opinion count?

A sense of inadequacy in individual participants can distract attention from the topic. The "I" needs to feel safe and accepted, and the "We" needs to emerge as a group, in order that the group can focus on the "It".

Tips for facilitators

Create space at the beginning for "I" and "We". Start with a round of introductions if participants do not yet know each other (ask them just to give names and say a single sentence about themselves if you are short of time). Allow participants to feel comfortable with each other. Although this will take some time from the issues you are working on, the investment will be worthwhile as the group will be better able to focus on the topic later on and discussions will be more productive.

Experiential learning

Experiential learning means learning through experience or discovery. It is a transformative process during which learners acquire new skills, new attitudes and new ways of thinking. It engages our head, heart and hands, and provides opportunities to take the initiative, make decisions and accept responsibility.

Experiential learning is based on a number of principles that youth workers or facilitators should try to follow when running educational activities or taking action with young people.

The cycle of experiential learning

All the educational activities in the T-Kit are based on the cycle of experiential learning (see Figure 8), which follows the process described below:

- ▶ the process starts with doing an activity as described in the instructions (Phase 1: Experiencing);
- ▶ this is followed by a debriefing that encourages young people to reflect on what has happened and how they felt (Phase 2: Reflecting);
- ▶ the facilitator then encourages participants to evaluate how this experience relates to the real world, and provides relevant information about the issue they are discussing (Phase 3: Generalising);
- ▶ finally, the young people and the youth worker consider different suggestions for follow-up, so that the learners can apply what they have learned to their reality, and implement an action that might make a difference to their community (Phase 4: Applying).

Taking action as a tool for experiential learning

The learning process continues to progress in a spiralling manner (see Figure 8) even when the young people leave the classroom, youth centre or other learning space. Inspired by experience-based educational activities, young people may decide to take actions to address the issues that are most important for them.

The spiral of experiential learning

Figure 8. The experiential learning process

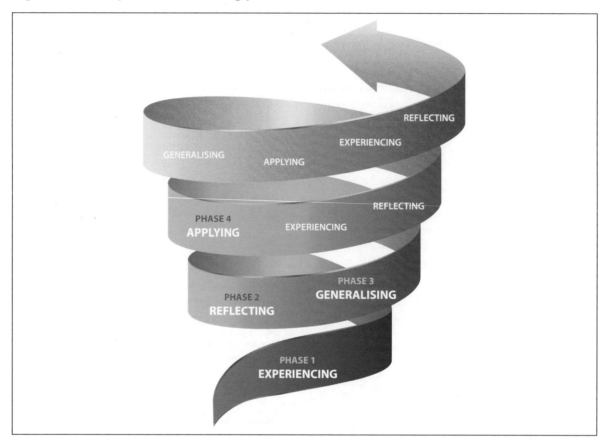

Principles of experiential learning

Experiential learning draws on the following principles (adapted from Chapman, McPhee P. and Proudman 1995):

▶ a mixture of content and process: try to keep a good balance between process-oriented activities and information/theoretical input;

▶ absence of excessive judgment: try to create a safe space for learning and abstain from interfering with participants' process of self-discovery. It is important to let young people have their own experiences without feeling they may be judged;

▶ engagement in purposeful endeavours: youth workers have to recognise the learner-as-teacher, and acknowledge a group's ability to provide coaching and mentoring to each other. The learning must be personally relevant and meaningful;

▶ encouraging the "big picture" perspective: experiential learning provides opportunities for young people to experience their relationship with a broader world. Educational activities should strengthen young people's ability to interact with complex systems and understand the interconnectedness of all things;

▶ teaching with multiple learning styles: experiential learning includes a cycle of all four learning styles: experiencing, reflective observation, generalisation (or conceptualisation) and application (see Figure 8);

▶ the role of reflection: reflection helps young people to pay attention to their own learning and gain insights about themselves and about their relationship to the world at large;

▶ creating emotional investment: the youth worker's challenge is to create a physically and emotionally safe environment where young people can be fully immersed in the learning experience;

▶ a re-examination of values: personal transformational growth is at the heart of experiential learning. Young people are invited to re-examine and explore their own values in a safe and supportive environment;

▶ the presence of meaningful relationships: experiential learning is not an abstract process, it is experienced as a series of relationships: learner to self, learner to teacher and learner to learning environment;

▶ learning outside the comfort zone: young people learn best when they are given the opportunity to explore outside their perceived comfort zone. Learning should not bring discomfort or insecurity, but it should challenge learners to open up to new experiences and step out of their comfort zone.

USING THE ACTIVITIES

Choosing the right educational activity depends on knowing your group and knowing the activities well. There are many which will be suitable for your group, and with a small amount of adaptation, almost any can be made to fit. Look for issues or methodologies which your group is likely to respond to, clarify your objectives for the session, and make sure that your selected activity is at the appropriate level in terms of experience and ability.

Familiarise yourself with the table of educational activities at the beginning of Chapter 4 and use the brief summaries to identify activities that are likely to work for your group.

Level of complexity

The activities have been divided according to three levels of complexity:

▶ Level 1: these are short and simple activities. They are useful as an introduction, so participants can get to know each other and you can gain a picture of participants' awareness of and concern about the issue of sustainability;

▶ Level 2: these activities are a little more complex and develop a deeper understanding of an issue. They may require more time;

▶ Level 3: these activities are longer, require good group work and discussion skills, concentration and co-operation from the participants, and may involve more preparation. They provide a wider and deeper understanding of the issues.

If you are meeting a particular group for the first time, select a Level 1 activity and use this to assess the knowledge, experience and interests of the group.

Time

An estimate of the time needed for the activity is provided in the table of educational activities. This time estimate includes the debriefing, but not the suggestions for follow-up or action. However, you should note that the estimated time allows for some flexibility: often a smaller group will require less time, and sometimes you may find that a lively discussion needs more time either at the end of the session or as a follow-up. The timings should be used as guidance only.

Instructions

The activities aim to be self-explanatory and the detailed instructions guide you through the different stages. You should always read these instructions carefully beforehand   at least twice – so that you understand clearly how the activity progresses and what is required from you as facilitator. You should also take careful note of the section "Preparation": make sure you check that you have all that is needed to run the activity.

Debriefing

The debriefing is an important part of the activity as a whole, and should not be missed out. There are guiding questions to help the facilitator conduct the debriefing and evaluation, but you should feel free to change these questions if others seem more appropriate. Even if you do not use your own questions, do not feel it is necessary to use all the listed questions: select a few, and make sure these are discussed properly by the group.

Tips for facilitators

Some of the activities contain some additional guidance notes which might indicate things to be aware of when running the activity. Make sure you read them carefully.

Suggestions for follow-up

This section indicates other activities in the manual that are related or raise similar points.

Ideas for action

Recalling the experiential cycle, this is an important part of the learning process and you should try to put aside some time to work through suggestions for action, and to debrief these afterwards. Look at the chapter "Making a difference" for further ideas and guidance.

Background resources

Many of the activities contain background information to support the facilitators in identifying the main issues that the activity is likely to raise and gain a better understanding of the topic.

Budapest Go Green

A group of young environmentalists in Hungary made an alternative map of Budapest called "Budapest Go Green". They gathered information about green living places in the city, including:

- ▶ organic shops;
- ▶ fair-trade shops and restaurants;
- ▶ vegetarian and fair-trade restaurants;
- ▶ second-hand shops and flea markets;
- ▶ farmers' markets;
- ▶ repair shops (to fix household items);
- ▶ bicycle renting and repair places;
- ▶ environmental non-governmental organisations.

They published and distributed a small booklet in Hungarian and English aiming to help locals and visitors "enjoy the green side of Budapest map indicating these places".

Chapter 4
Activities

SUMMARY OF ACTIVITIES

	Name	Level	Time/min	Group size	Overview	Page
1	A finite planet	1	45	Any	This is a discussion activity, where participants take a stand on a series of statements relating mostly to consumerism and the competitive economy.	26
2	Chain reactions	2	60	6-30	Participants explore the causes and effects of climate change by arranging and ordering cause–effect cards.	29
3	Chicken sandwich	3	60-80	10-25	Using information cards, participants analyse the environmental impact of a shop-bought chicken sandwich.	34
4	Climate superhero auditions	1	60	7-30	Using role play, participants construct arguments for including different communities or professional bodies in a "climate superhero team".	40
5	Fishing game	3	90-120	10-30	This is a simulation activity in two parts that helps to introduce the concept of sustainable fishing.	43
6	Greenwashing	3	90-120	4-30	Participants analyse advertisements to identify the false messaging at the heart of greenwashing. They use creative skills to develop their own awareness-raising advertisements against environmental threats.	48
7	How big is my foot?	2	60	Any	Participants calculate their ecological footprint and discuss the sustainable lifestyle changes we can make to decrease our footprints.	52
8	Mapping the globe	3	90	9-20	This activity uses mind-mapping to point up the connections between human rights and the environment.	61
9	Nature journalists	1	60-90	Any	This is an outdoor activity that aims to recreate a sense of connection with nature and the environment.	66

10	Needs and wants	1	45	Any	This activity looks at the difference between needs and wants, how we define each, and why this matters for the planet's sustainability.	68
11	NeoClear Inc.	3	120	10-20	This is a simulation exercise exploring different opinions on nuclear energy and sustainability.	72
12	Our futures	2	60	6+	This is a creative activity, where participants design and draw a model for an ideal development in their community.	78
13	Stop climate chaos	1	45	12+	This is a lively introductory activity in which participants learn about climate change through a competitive teamwork game.	82
14	Sustainability bingo	1	15-30	12+	This is an introductory activity for participants to get to know each other and tune in to the topic of sustainability.	85
15	Take a step forward	2	60	10-30	In this activity participants take on roles and move forward depending on their chances and opportunities in life.	88
16	The cost of fashion	3	50	6+	Participants learn about the "cost" of a cotton T-shirt, and then go on to plan an action to address the related environmental issues.	94
17	Thumbs up, thumbs down	1	15-30	Any	This is a physical activity to spark a discussion on the difference between competition and collaboration.	99
18	Waste manifesto	2	100	6-30	This activity raises awareness about the problem of pollution and waste.	101

A FINITE PLANET

Overview

This is a discussion activity, where participants take a stand on a series of statements mostly relating to consumerism and the competitive economy.

Key concepts

Consumerism, capitalism, growth, competition, economy

Complexity: Level 1

Group size: Any

Time: 45 minutes

Objectives

- to reflect on the relationship between commonly held views about the economy and the question of sustainability;
- to engage in discussion and practise communication skills;
- to question assumptions commonly accepted in capitalist society.

Preparation

Prepare two posters – one saying "Agree" and the other saying "Disagree" – and stick them on the floor at opposite ends of the room, so that people can form a straight line between them. You may want to draw a chalk line between them, or use a piece of string.

Instructions

1. Point out the signs "Agree" and "Disagree" and ask participants to stand somewhere along the line between them.

2. Explain that you will read out a series of statements, and participants should position themselves along the line, according to how much they agree or disagree with the statement. They should try to stand near others whose views are close to their own.

3. Select from the list of statements those which you think are most relevant or interesting for your group. Start reading them out, allowing some time between each one for a brief discussion, and so that participants can reposition themselves. Ask a few people why they are standing where they are, and allow others to change their position if they find the arguments presented convincing.

4. Read out the statements in turn.

5. After 20-30 minutes, bring the group back together for the debriefing.

Debriefing

- Which statement was most difficult for you to position yourself according to?
- Were there any questions where you changed your position as a result of something someone else said?
- Which statement led to the most disagreement, and can you explain this?
- Do you think people in your country would mostly agree with the statements? Does that mean they must be true?
- How do you think we come to learn such common beliefs? How do we help to spread them? How are they reinforced?
- What relevance do these beliefs have to the question of sustainability? Is it possible to have limitless growth on a finite planet?

- Does an end to "growth" have to mean standing still? How could we continue to improve the life of humankind without continuing to take more from the planet's finite resources?
- Do you think you have any beliefs which are not compatible with the idea of a sustainable planet?

Tips for facilitators

Allow sufficient time between each statement for participants to listen to each other's views and reflect on different opinions – and perhaps, to change positions.

Try to give everyone a chance to comment on the position they have occupied. You could ask those at the end-points to explain why they have occupied an extreme position, or ask someone near the centre whether their position indicates a lack of a strong opinion or lack of knowledge.

Suggestions for follow-up

A more structured debating activity can be found in "NeoClear Inc.", which looks at the arguments for and against nuclear power.

If you want to develop young people's sensitivity towards nature, you could try the activity "Nature journalists".

Ideas for action

Encourage young people to consider the news outlets they usually read. Are there any hidden assumptions? Are these assumptions incompatible with a sustainable future for the planet? Support them to question the journalists making these assumptions: on social media, or in a letter, by e-mail. Encourage your group to realise that it is important that journalists see themselves as "accountable" to their readers – and also that they begin to question their own assumptions!

Handout: statements for the activity

Select those which are more relevant for your group – you do not have to use all the statements!

More is always better

Time is money

Money makes the world go around

A healthy society depends on a growing economy

We do not need to lower our energy consumption: science will find a solution for green energy sources available on a mass scale

Competition makes us better

Private companies provide better public services, such as education, health care and transportation, than public institutions

Free market competition promotes creativity and efficiency

Natural resources (e.g. water, coal, oil, fish and forests) exist to satisfy human needs

We deserve cheap electricity and cheap fuel for our cars

We cannot change the current economic system – it is the only model that works

The only people who care about the environment are hippies (tree huggers) who want to stop economic development

A car is an excellent means of transportation, it is impossible to live without it

I am not interested in environmentalism. I just want to live my life

CHAIN REACTIONS

This activity is an adaptation of "Chain reactions" from the resource pack "The Sustainable Development Goals and youth", National Youth Council of Ireland (2015)

Overview

Participants explore the causes and effects of climate change by arranging and ordering a set of cause–effect cards.

Key concepts

Climate change, causes and effects, extreme weather events, personal responsibility

Complexity: Level 2

Group size: 6-30

Time: 60 minutes

Objectives

▶ to learn about the causes and effects of climate change;
▶ to practise critical thinking skills;
▶ to consider personal contributions to climate change and how these affect others.

Materials

Sets of cards at the end of the activity

Preparation

Copy and cut out the three chains. You will need 1 set (or chain) for each small group.

Instructions

1. Divide participants into groups of 8. In each group, give each participant one card at random from one of the chains at the end of the activity. Explain that each group of 8 has to form a human chain, so that each card – and the person holding it – follows on from the one before. If it is hard to divide the group into smaller groups of 8, ask participants to lay out the cards in sequence on the floor or table. Groups can then be almost any size.

2. When one group forms a chain, announce it as the winner, and then check with the whole group that the cards follow on correctly. Ask participants to remain in their chain and read the cards aloud in sequence.

3. Check the results of the other two groups in the same way, or complete those chains, if necessary, with the help of all participants.

4. Point out that the chains link the lives of young people with people in other parts of the world. Ask what the element is which links the cards together: how are the people in the first cards connected to those in the last?

5. Give them some information about climate change from the background information included here. Then use some of the questions below to explore their reactions to the information and to the activity itself.

Debriefing

▶ How easy was it to get the cards in the right order? What made it difficult? Which clues did you use to help organise them?

- Did anything about the activity surprise you?
- Which actions in your own lives contribute towards climate change?
- Do you think any of the items in the list could be reduced or eliminated (in your lives)? How?

Remind participants that although small, the initial actions at the beginning of each of the chains have a significant impact on the amount of carbon dioxide in the atmosphere because they are actions undertaken by many millions of people – particularly in the richer countries. They do not really represent single actions – for example, a single journey to a local school – they represent many millions of journeys to millions of local schools.

Tips for facilitators

If you have a large group, make extra copies of the cards, and use some of the chains twice; if you work with a smaller group, use just 1 or 2 of the chains.

When the groups have finished, even if you were not able to form groups of 8, you can still illustrate the chain effect in the reporting back of groups. Ask the reporting group to stand in a chain of 8 people, with each person holding a card. Card holders can be borrowed from other groups for this part of the activity. Then ask the card holders to read out the cards in order (while still linked to each other).

Suggestions for follow-up

The activity "How big is my foot?" measures participants' ecological footprints by means of a questionnaire. This is a good way for them to assess their own contribution to climate change.

You could also follow up with the activity "Climate superhero auditions", which looks at the role of different sectors in campaigning against climate change.

Ideas for action

The group could take the list of its own contributions, drawn up at the end of the activity, and use this to draw up individual action plans. You could also explore as a group whether there are things the youth centre could do to reduce its carbon emissions. If this is dependent on the local council or another body – e.g. if they provide heating to the whole building – think about how you could involve other users of the building.

Background information – Climate change: what is it all about?

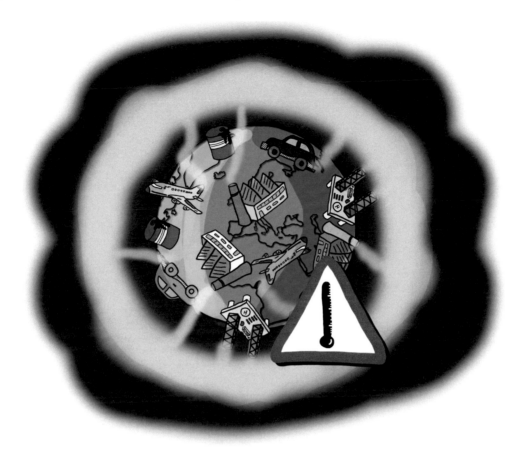

The following provides a brief on climate change:

► climate change is caused by the release of too much carbon dioxide and other gases into the earth's atmosphere. The gases form a blanket around the earth that traps heat. These gases are released when we use fuels such as petrol, gas and coal, or electricity from these sources; in the last 130 years, the world has warmed by approximately 0.85 °C. Each of the last three decades has been successively warmer than any preceding decade since 1850. Higher temperatures lead to a rise in sea levels, melting glaciers, and an increase in extreme weather events, including floods, hurricanes and droughts;

► rich countries contribute far more than poor countries to climate change because they use more energy in their homes, businesses and factories;

► most rich countries have also historically contributed far more to the amount of carbon dioxide in the atmosphere: they began to develop their industries at a time when people did not know about the effects of burning carbon fuels. Most of the excess carbon dioxide in the atmosphere was put there by the richer countries;

► the effects of climate change are felt most by poor people in developing countries, where hurricanes, floods, drought and malaria affect their livelihoods and health;

► in the year 2000, the World Health Organization (WHO) estimated that about 150 000 people die as a result of climate change every year. By 2020, that will be a total of about 3 million climate deaths. WHO has now revised its estimate, and believes that between 2030 and 2050, climate change will cause approximately 250 000 additional deaths per year, from malnutrition, malaria, diarrhoea and heat stress;

► extreme high air temperatures contribute directly to deaths from heart disease and respiratory disease, particularly among elderly people. In the heat wave of the summer of 2003 in Europe, for example, more than 70 000 excess deaths were recorded (www.who.int/mediacentre/factsheets/fs266/en/).

Figure 9. Deaths from climate change (CC deaths)

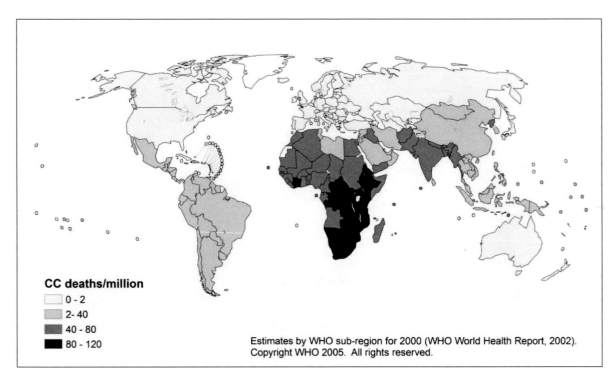

CC deaths/million
0 - 2
2 - 40
40 - 80
80 - 120

Estimates by WHO sub-region for 2000 (WHO World Health Report, 2002).

Source: World Health Organization, www.who.int/heli/risks/climate/climatechange/en/

Handout: chain reaction cards

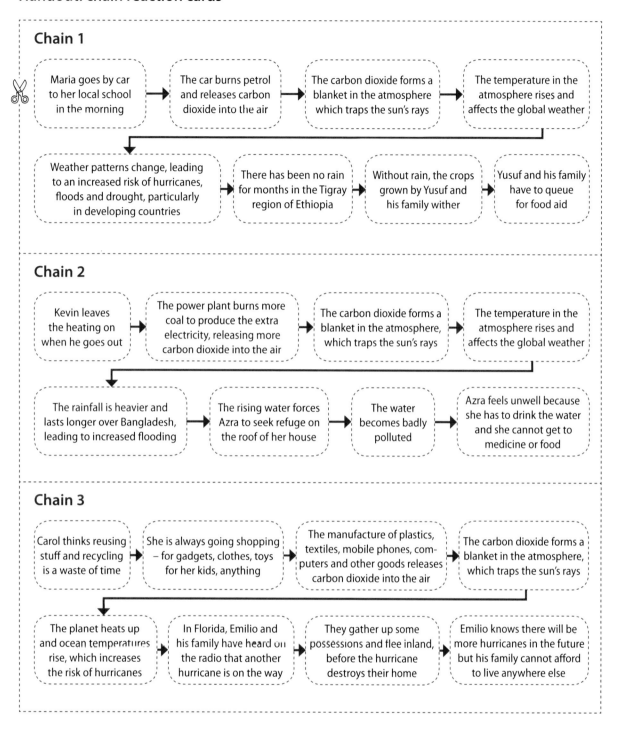

Chain 1

Maria goes by car to her local school in the morning → The car burns petrol and releases carbon dioxide into the air → The carbon dioxide forms a blanket in the atmosphere which traps the sun's rays → The temperature in the atmosphere rises and affects the global weather →

Weather patterns change, leading to an increased risk of hurricanes, floods and drought, particularly in developing countries → There has been no rain for months in the Tigray region of Ethiopia → Without rain, the crops grown by Yusuf and his family wither → Yusuf and his family have to queue for food aid

Chain 2

Kevin leaves the heating on when he goes out → The power plant burns more coal to produce the extra electricity, releasing more carbon dioxide into the air → The carbon dioxide forms a blanket in the atmosphere, which traps the sun's rays → The temperature in the atmosphere rises and affects the global weather →

The rainfall is heavier and lasts longer over Bangladesh, leading to increased flooding → The rising water forces Azra to seek refuge on the roof of her house → The water becomes badly polluted → Azra feels unwell because she has to drink the water and she cannot get to medicine or food

Chain 3

Carol thinks reusing stuff and recycling is a waste of time → She is always going shopping – for gadgets, clothes, toys for her kids, anything → The manufacture of plastics, textiles, mobile phones, computers and other goods releases carbon dioxide into the air → The carbon dioxide forms a blanket in the atmosphere, which traps the sun's rays →

The planet heats up and ocean temperatures rise, which increases the risk of hurricanes → In Florida, Emilio and his family have heard on the radio that another hurricane is on the way → They gather up some possessions and flee inland, before the hurricane destroys their home → Emilio knows there will be more hurricanes in the future but his family cannot afford to live anywhere else

CHICKEN SANDWICH

Overview

Using information cards, participants analyse the environmental impact of a shop-bought chicken sandwich.

Key concepts

Food, health, agriculture, biodiversity, factory farming, multinational corporations

Complexity: Level 3

Group size: 10-25

Time: Part 1: 60 minutes; Part 2: 20 minutes

Objectives

- ▶ to explore the links between food and sustainability;
- ▶ to learn about some of the food-related threats to the environment and human health;
- ▶ to reflect on our own eating and purchasing practices.

Materials

- ▶ "chicken club sandwich" and cards on page 37-39.

Preparation

For Part 1:

- ▶ make copies of "chicken club sandwich". You will need at least one copy for each small group (4-6 people);
- ▶ copy the cards and cut them up. Each small group needs 11 cards, randomly distributed. If you have more than 12 participants, make another copy of the cards and distribute these among the remaining groups (11 cards for each group);
- ▶ optional: stick the "chicken club sandwich" on a larger piece of paper, so participants can fix their cards around it. You will then need sticky tape or Blu-Tack for each group.

For Part 2 (optional):

- ▶ ask participants to bring in a favourite item of food, or something they eat very regularly. They could also bring in the label, if the food is packaged.

Instructions

Part 1

1. Divide participants into groups of 4-6 people. Hand out sets of 11 cards to each small group, and a copy of the "chicken sandwich" page.

2. Ask participants to distribute the cards among members of their group. It does not matter if some people have more cards.

3. For the first few minutes, ask them to read the cards they have received, and study the ingredients listed on the "chicken sandwich" handout. In silence, participants should place any cards which might be relevant to the chicken sandwich around the sheet. When they have finished, they should look at the cards placed by other people in their group.

4. After about 5 minutes of silently placing cards and reading those placed by others, ask participants to discuss the following questions in their groups:
   - were you surprised by how many of the cards were relevant to the chicken sandwich?

- would any of these cards put you off eating this sandwich (or put you off eating something with similar ingredients)?
- which was the most shocking or surprising card?

5. Give them 20-30 minutes to discuss the cards, then invite groups back for brief presentations. As the groups have been discussing different cards, they will need to read out any relevant cards for other groups.

6. After the presentations, debrief this part of the activity (see below).

Part 2 (optional)

7. Display the 10 questions from the handout on page 39 on a flip chart or screen. Ask participants to answer the questions on their own, using the piece of food they brought in. If they cannot answer any of the questions, they should write "not known".

8. Give them a few minutes for this exercise, then use some of the questions in the second debriefing (see below).

Debriefing

Part 1

- ▶ How do you feel at the end of this activity?
- ▶ Are you surprised by how little we tend to know about the food we eat?
- ▶ Do you think that we should know more? Why, or why not?
- ▶ Have your opinions changed from the beginning of the activity?
- ▶ Will you make any changes in your own eating habits?
- ▶ What could we do as a group or community to address some of the problems discussed today?

Part 2

- ▶ Could anyone answer all the questions?
- ▶ Could anyone answer any of them? Do you think the questions are important? Why, or why not?
- ▶ Which ones are most important? Would the answer to any of them make a difference to whether you will go on eating that food?
- ▶ Discuss some of the answers participants wrote down.

Tips for facilitators

If you stick the handout onto a large piece of flip chart paper, and give the groups some sticky tape, they could stick their cards around the sandwich, creating a visual collage. Before the sharing, groups could then look at the results of the other groups.

Some participants may be a little resistant to the "bad" news about favourite foods contained on the cards, e.g. the information about the meat industry. The purpose of the activity is not necessarily to make everyone change their eating habits! It is to open participants' minds to the fact that our eating choices do have consequences, and to encourage them to be more thoughtful and aware of these consequences.

It is important at the end to come up with some positive ideas for the group so that the participants feel they can make a contribution to some of the problems discussed. See the ideas for action.

Suggestions for follow-up

The activity "Fishing game" is a simulation, looking at the sustainability of our oceans and the effects of commercial fishing.

You could also follow up by looking at "Waste manifesto", which examines the different types of waste and associated problems.

The activity "The cost of fashion" moves beyond food, and examines the clothing industry, including social and environmental conditions in manufacturing countries.

The following websites served as sources for the food sustainability cards. Encourage participants to explore these sites – and others – to supplement the information provided:

- ▶ www.greenpeace.org/usa/sustainable-agriculture/issues/corporate-control
- ▶ http://worldinfo.org
- ▶ www.onegreenplanet.org
- ▶ www.plasticoceans.org/the-facts
- ▶ www.dosomething.org
- ▶ http://ec.europa.eu/environment/archives/eussd/food.htm
- ▶ www.worldwildlife.org/threats/overfishing
- ▶ www.vegsoc.org/saveland

Ideas for action

There are numerous ways to take action to make food systems more sustainable:

- ▶ make posters featuring some of the information that participants felt was most important, and use these for an awareness-raising campaign locally;
- ▶ researching and creating a map of local and sustainable food producers;
- ▶ getting a group allotment or finding a plot of land for the group to begin growing its own food;
- ▶ organising an event where sustainable local food is cooked and shared;
- ▶ building a compost bin and starting to compost food scraps;
- ▶ contacting a local or national NGO that works on the issue of food sustainability and asking them to speak to the group, or about ways that the group could contribute to their work.

Handout for Part 1: food sustainability cards

The world produces nearly 300 million tonnes of plastic every year, half of which is for single use. More than 8 million tonnes of plastic are dumped into our oceans every year. If this continues, there will be more plastic than fish in the ocean by 2050.

There are already more than 5 trillion pieces of plastic in the world's oceans, most of them microplastics. These tiny broken-down pieces of plastic look like food to fish: they can end up killing the fish, or a bird which eats the fish. Some have been found in fish eaten by humans.

Between a third and a half of all food produced around the world is lost or wasted. This is about 2 billion tonnes of food. In the EU, food waste is expected to rise to about 126 million tonnes a year by 2020.

The average Western diet has high levels of meat, fat and sugar, which carries risks for individual health, and for the health system. Obesity, type 2 diabetes, hypertension, osteoarthritis, and cancer are widespread diet-related diseases.

Recent decades have seen a trend towards less sustainable and less healthy diets. For the first time in history, the world has as many overweight people as undernourished people.

More than 85% of the world's fisheries are either beyond, or up to safe biological limits. The populations of several fish populations (such as Atlantic bluefin tuna) have shrunk to the point where their survival as a species is threatened.

Greenhouse gas emissions relating to the food we eat are partly a result of transport costs, but mostly a result of the way the food is produced – e.g. by industrial methods or by hand, in heated greenhouses or in open fields, on existing land, or land cleared from forest.

Many countries in the developing world have deals with rich donor countries that force small farmers to shift to industrial farming methods. These arrangements tell the farmers what to plant: mostly crops for far-off markets instead of local crops to feed people at home.

Agriculture is one of the biggest threats to a healthy environment. It uses most of our available freshwater, and about 20 000-50 000 square kilometres of potentially productive land is lost annually through unsustainable farming methods resulting in soil erosion and degradation.

A typical meat eater's diet requires up to 2.5 times the amount of land compared to a vegetarian diet and five times that of a vegan diet.

A farmer can feed up to 30 people throughout the year with vegetables, fruits, cereals and vegetable fats on 1 hectare of land. If the same area is used for the production of eggs, milk and/or meat the number of people fed is about 5-10.

The meat industry accounts for 14% of greenhouse gas emissions worldwide, which is roughly equivalent to all emissions from transport.

The cattle industry is responsible for up to 80% of Amazon deforestation. The Amazon is home to at least 10% of the world's known biodiversity and plays an essential role in regulation of the planet's climate.

Livestock is the most significant contributor to nitrogen and phosphorus pollution of streams, rivers and coastal waters worldwide.

Four multinational corporations control between 75-90% of the global grain trade. Corporations are exerting increasing pressure on farmers, making them grow crops which can be easily traded, like corn and soy, instead of native crops.

Six enormous agribusiness companies control nearly 70% of the world's seed market. The same companies control all the genetically modified (GM) crops, whose effects on the environment – and on humans – are largely untested. Again, these 6 companies are the largest global manufacturers of pesticides.

Many of the foods we eat every day are sprayed with pesticides before they land on our tables. There are a growing number of studies that have linked certain pesticides with increased cancer risk and with diseases such as Parkinson's and Alzheimer's.

30-40% of all food is wasted, At every step of the food cycle, 30-40% of all food is wasted. Each year, a large proportion of the food produced in developing countries never makes it to market. Consumers in rich countries waste as much food as the entire net food production of sub-Saharan Africa.

For centuries, peasant farmers have always put aside a small portion of their crop as the following year's seed. Now, large multinational corporations often prevent farmers from saving seeds, forcing them to buy new seeds for every planting season.

Factory farms now account for 72% of poultry production, 43% of egg production, and 55% of pork production worldwide. Factory farms contribute to air pollution by releasing compounds such as hydrogen sulphide, ammonia and methane.

Factory farms normally store animal waste in huge, open-air lagoons, often as big as several football fields, which are prone to leaks and spills. In 2011, an Illinois hog farm spilled 200 000 gallons of manure into a creek, killing over 110 000 fish.

Land clearing in Brazil to grow chicken feed is responsible for the destruction of about 3 million acres of rainforest. Land clearing to grow soybeans in the Amazon rainforest is responsible for clearing over 100 million hectares of forest, destroying soil fertility, threatening biodiversity, polluting freshwater and displacing communities.

Part 2: Questions (for display on flip chart or overhead projector)

▶ Where is your food from? Has it travelled far to get to your plate?

▶ Is the food nutritious, good for your health?

▶ Is there any packaging? Is the packaging recyclable?

▶ Do you know how the food was made? Was a lot of machinery used?

▶ Were any pesticides or other chemicals used in producing it?

▶ Was any waste produced in making this food?

▶ Are there any other costs to the environment in the production of this food?

▶ What proportion of the price of this food went to those who made it (or grew it)?

▶ Who else made money out of this food?

▶ Are there other foods or other methods of production which would have a better impact on the environment?

CLIMATE SUPERHERO AUDITIONS

This activity is an adaptation from the teaching pack "Heat up over climate change", UNICEF.

Overview

Using role play, participants construct arguments for including different communities or professional bodies in a "climate superhero team".

Key concepts

Climate change, activism, society, democracy

Complexity: Level 1

Group size: Any (small groups 6-8)

Time: 60 minutes

Objectives

- ▶ to understand the contribution of different elements of society in combating climate change;
- ▶ to practice presentation and argumentation skills;
- ▶ to appreciate the importance of one's own contribution.

Materials

- ▶ character cards;
- ▶ space to carry out the auditions;
- ▶ optional: materials such as paper and coloured pens for the groups' presentations.

Preparation

Copy and cut out the character cards. Each small group gets a different card (character): the groups will need enough copies of one of the cards for all members.

Instructions

If you have not previously worked on climate change with the group, you could give it some information from pages 31-32 or begin by asking it to brainstorm what its members already know, and why the matter urgently needs addressing.

1. Ask the group to imagine it is interviewing potential candidates to join the climate change superhero dream team.

2. Divide them into seven smaller groups, but explain that the entire group will be the interviewing panel.

3. Give each group one of the character cards. The whole group will be that character and will need to convince the interview panel (the rest of the group) why they should be the ones to join the climate change superhero dream team.

4. Give groups 10-15 minutes to prepare – as a group – a 2-minute drama, speech or presentation for the interview panel. Groups will need to think about why their character is essential to combating climate change, and why he/she can make the most valuable contribution.

5. After about 15 minutes, get the group together and announce the start of the climate superhero auditions. Remind them that they all represent the judges (as well as their own characters). Tell them that there will be 4 places on the team and they cannot vote for their own character!

6. Give each group (character) 2 minutes to convince the rest of the group why they should be on the team.

7.   When everyone has done their presentation, announce the voting. Tell them they can vote as an individual, but remind them not to vote for their group's character. They can choose four characters in total that they would like to be on the team.

8.   Read out the names of the seven characters in turn, taking votes for each one. The four characters who receive the most votes will be the ones on the superhero team.

9.   Announce the winning characters!

Debriefing

Begin by asking for participants' general impressions: what did they think of the activity and were they happy with the final make-up of the team? Then use some of the following questions to lead the group towards some ideas for action.

▸ Do you think the team would be better if all the characters were members? Why or why not?

▸ Do you think that in real life, the group which you represented does enough to fight against climate change? Or do representatives of this group make the fight more difficult?

▸ Are there other characters/roles (not discussed today) that you think should be included in a team to fight climate change? Ask participants to list others they would include;

▸ How many people do you think it would really take to deal with the problem of climate change? Is a "team" of people enough for such a task?

▸ Are there things that everyone in the world – no matter their role – can do to tackle climate change?

▸ What could you do? What could we do as a group?

End the session by making a list of the ways in which participants can help to address the problem of climate change. This might include making changes in their own lives, or it might include ideas for campaigning or lobbying or joining with other organisations.

Suggestions for follow-up

The activity "Greenwashing" looks at the way that many businesses not only do not play a proper role in fighting climate change, they actually cover up environmental damage, presenting a false view of the "good" they are doing.

"How big is my foot?" and "Chain reactions" also look at climate change.

Your group could look at the next section for some ideas on how to involve other groups in society in campaigning against climate change.

Ideas for action

Your group could take one or more of the groups or communities listed in the activity, and research what, if anything, they are doing to address climate change. For example:

▸ what is the position of the main parliamentary groups on climate change?

▸ can we invite a representative of one of these groups to speak to the group?

▸ do news outlets leave the question of climate change to the "environmental correspondent", or do all journalists take it into account? Are floods or other extreme events reported as a probable effect of climate change, or merely as "natural disasters"?

▸ can the group make contact with journalists to ensure they are playing their superhero role!?

▸ are local businesses taking their environmental responsibilities seriously? What is the effect of their business on the local environment, and on global environmental issues?

▸ can the group make contact with someone to question them about their role?

Handout: characters cards

Journalists

You can help uncover the real situation and tell others! You can keep the pressure on governments and scientists by reporting on progress. You can also tell the world about communities already affected by climate change and highlight where support and assistance is needed.

But – people could ignore what you say, the newspaper you work for might not be interested in printing the story or not enough people might read what you write.

Young people and communities

You can reduce your carbon impact by making changes to the way you live. You can keep pressure on businesses and governments to make sure they are doing everything in their power to reduce the carbon impact of your country. You can also campaign or raise money to ensure that communities around the world are given the support they need to deal with the effects of climate change.

But – you need time, commitment and perseverance. And not everyone might be interested.

Politicians

You have the power to make important decisions and laws that can limit the amount of carbon businesses are allowed to produce. You can make sure any cars in your country are fuel efficient. You can invest money to support scientists to innovate and come up with new green technology.

But – elections are coming up and you do not want to make any changes that will make you unpopular (like charging people more to fly by aeroplane). You want to stay in power. And, even without the elections looming, there may be a lack of public support for bold decisions!

Scientists

You can make new discoveries and invent new ways of producing energy that produce no carbon. Your inventions could revolutionise the world. You could also come up with things that will help communities already affected by climate change deal with their situation.

But – you rely on funding from governments and businesses, and you can only explore the things they ask you to. Plus your inventions will take years to develop and will need to be tested before they can be produced.

Business leaders

You have massive power to make changes. If you are a car manufacturer you could make sure all your cars are fuel efficient. Or if you are an electricity company you could build wind farms instead of coal-powered generators. This would have a massive impact on the world's carbon footprint!

But – you have to make as much money as possible for your shareholders, or else you will lose your job.

Campaigners and activists

You can research what governments and businesses are doing to address climate change, and you can campaign and lobby for them to do more. You can encourage communities to get involved – and give them the tools to contact their members of parliament to keep the pressure on governments to make important decisions on climate change.

But – you have very little money to support your efforts. People might not listen to you. You might be going against very wealthy and powerful people.

Charity workers

You can help the communities already facing the devastating effects of climate change. You can provide mosquito nets and training for people who are not used to dealing with malaria (because of climate change more areas are now facing the threat of malaria, a disease that is spread by mosquitoes). You can support communities to find solutions to water and food shortages. You can also use your influence to lobby governments and businesses to cut carbon emissions.

But – there are so many problems you are already dealing with, like supporting efforts against poverty and HIV. And you only have a limited amount of money and staff. You get funding from individual donations, businesses and governments, none of which is guaranteed to continue at the same levels.

FISHING GAME

This lesson is an adaptation of "Sustainable fishing", California Academy of Sciences.

Overview

This activity is a simulation of the fishing trade used to explore reasons for the decline in fish populations. Participants then explore ways of making fisheries more sustainable both for animals and the people who depend on them.

Key concepts

Fishing, sustainability, competition, consumerism, greed

Complexity: Level 3

Group size: 10-30

Time: 90-120 minutes

Objectives

- ▶ to understand environmental concerns related to over-fishing;
- ▶ to construct explanations and design solutions for maintaining healthy oceans;
- ▶ to appreciate the ways in which individuals can address the problem of declining fish populations.

Materials

- ▶ you will need 2 different types/shapes of small biscuits, sweets, or some other small object to represent the different fish;
    - – about 100 "goldfish" per small group;
    - – about 50 "turtles" per small group;
    - – about 100 pieces of popcorn per small group, to represent "other fish";
- ▶ 1 serving bowl or dinner plate per small group;
- ▶ 1 small cup per participant;
- ▶ spoons, 1 per participant;
- ▶ spatulas, 1 per group;
- ▶ tongs or chopsticks, 1 per group;
- ▶ a stopwatch, for timing the activity,
- ▶ fishing logs (page 47), 1 per student.

Preparation

- ▶ make sure you have all the equipment listed above;
- ▶ make copies of the fishing logs. You will need to copy the whole page (2 tables) for each student;
- ▶ make two "oceans" for each group of 5-7 students: put 60 "goldfish", 30 "turtles", and 60 pieces of popcorn ("other fish") in a bowl.

Instructions

Part 1

1. Tell participants that 1 billion people around the world depend upon seafood for their primary source of protein. Explain that today we will be going fishing!

2. Divide them into groups of 5-7 people and give each group an ocean. They can choose a name for their ocean.

3. Give every participant their own "boat" (cup), "net" (spoon) and fishing log. Tell them they are fishers whose livelihood depends on catching fish. They need to catch seafood that they can sell at the seafood market.

4. Introduce them to the different types of fish in their oceans:
    – goldfish are the fish they need to catch;
    – turtles (and other endangered species) are "fish" whose populations are endangered;
    – popcorn represent all other fish;

5. Talk through or display the fishing rules:
    – when the fishing season starts, use your "net" (spoon) to catch "fish" from the "ocean" (bowl). Deposit your catch into your "boat" (cup);
    – you can only use your net! Fingers, hands or anything else are out of play;
    – goldfish are the target fish: these are the ones you can sell at the seafood market;
    – if any unwanted fish – popcorn or turtle crackers – end up in your net, you cannot return them to the ocean;
    – if you do not catch at least five goldfish in a fishing season, you will not be able to survive to the next one. You will have to miss the next season;
    – there will be at least four fishing seasons in total.

6. Announce the start of Fishing Season 1 and give participants 20 seconds to fish. Then announce the end of the season. Participants must stop fishing promptly! Note: if participants are not depleting their oceans, increase the "season" to 30 seconds.

7. Ask everyone to count their goldfish catch, other fish catch (popcorn), and endangered by-catch (such as sea turtles). The information should be recorded in the fishing logs.

8. While participants are recording their catch, and before the start of the next season:
    – go round each ocean adding a new goldfish for each one left in the ocean; a new endangered fish for each one left, and the same for the other fish. Explain that this represents natural reproduction of the remaining fish in the sea;
    – ask if anyone caught less than five goldfish, and tell them that they must miss the next season if so;
    – give 1 fisher in each group a spatula and tell them that this represents trawling, and they can use it in Season 2 instead of the spoon. You can give it to a different participant for Season 3.

9. Announce the start of Season 2, and repeat the same procedure as for Season 1:
    – fish for 20-30 seconds;
    – fill out the logs;
    – add to the oceans: one more of each kind of fish for each one remaining;
    – give a spatula to one participant in each group (only for Seasons 2 and 3).

10. Run Season 3 the same way as Season 2.

11. For Season 4, take away the spatula and give 1 participant in each group a set of tongs or chopsticks. This represents a hook and line.

12. Add extra seasons after Season 4, if needed, until all (or most) groups fish out their ocean. Note: if, or when a group fishes all the creatures in their ocean, allow it to "invade" other oceans. It may spread out to different oceans, or go as one group to a single ocean. Do not tell participants in advance that they can do this!

13. Bring the whole group together to debrief this part of the activity.

Debriefing (Part 1)

Use some of the following questions to talk about what happened and what participants observed.
  ▶ Which oceans ran out of fish? What were the main reasons?
  ▶ Which fishing methods caught the most fish?
  ▶ Which fishing methods resulted in most by-catch (fish other than the target fish)?

- Can you describe what happened in your ocean, over the full four seasons, with reference to your logs?
- What were you trying to do: were you thinking about catching as many fish as possible, or did you consider what it would mean if all the fishers tried to do that?
- How much of the activity represented the real fishing industry: which bits are realistic, and what might be missing from the model?

Give participants some information from the background information provided in "Sustainable fishing", then move on to Part 2.

Part 2

1. Divide participants back into their "ocean" groups and ask them to brainstorm how they might protect their ocean. They need to think about how to maintain healthy populations of fish that can continue to reproduce over generations to come, while still allowing fishers to make a living – and providing sufficient fish to those who survive on a diet of fish. Ask each group to write out its proposals and draw up a set of rules.

2. Fill up the oceans again and ask students to try out their ideas. Run the same number of seasons as previously.

Debriefing (Part 2)

Discuss differences between this round and the first.

- Did you have more or less fish left in the ocean at the end?
- Did you reduce the amount of by-catch?
- Did all your fishers "survive" all seasons?
- How did your own state of mind differ: were you more or less anxious to catch more fish?

Ask groups to outline briefly the proposals they came up with.

- Do you think your proposals were effective? Would you change anything in another game?
- Do you think these proposals would work in real life?

End the session by asking participants how they feel at the end of the whole activity.

- Do you think the activity was a true reflection of reality?
- Before the activity, were you aware of the problem of over-fishing? What do you think now?
- Will this activity make a difference to your behaviour? How?

Tips for facilitators

You can use fewer fish or different implements, but you may need to adjust the timings after the first round to make sure most of the fish are caught.

If you run out of "fish" to replenish the oceans, you can recycle those already caught by participants. Ask them to tip their fish into a general receptacle after they have counted them.

Suggestions for follow-up

If participants would like to learn more about food and sustainability, try the activity "Chicken sandwich". You could also use the activity "Mapping the globe", where participants use a mind map to explore the links between food, water and health in the context of human rights.

Ideas for action

Participants could carry out further research into the fish they eat, or the fish that are available in local shops and supermarkets. There are organisations which list the fish that are currently endangered – e.g. Worldwide Fund for Nature or Greenpeace (see www.greenpeace.org.uk/what-we-do/oceans/better-buys-what-fish-can-i-eat/sustainable-seafood-faqs/). Alternatively, participants could write a letter to local shops in the name of their youth group, asking for confirmation that fish sold are caught according to sustainable fishing practices.

Background information – Sustainable fishing

A sustainable fishery is one whose practices can be maintained indefinitely without reducing the targeted species' ability to maintain its population at healthy levels, and without adversely impacting on other species within the ecosystem – including humans – by removing their food source, accidentally killing them, or damaging their physical environment (Greenpeace, www.greenpeace.org/archive-international/en/campaigns/oceans/seafood/what-is-a-sustainable-fishery/).

Tuna over-fishing

Tuna are among the world's most popular fish, and for many coastal communities, a vital part of their diet, economy, and even culture. For centuries, people fished for tuna without disturbing the balance of life in the oceans. However, the era of industrial fishing with massive ships has led to more fish being caught than can be reproduced by those left behind. This results in gradual depletion of the fish population.

Industrial fishing boats can catch around 3 000 tonnes of tuna in a single trip. This is twice the amount that some Pacific Island nations take into their waters annually (Greenpeace 2012):

▸ in 1950, the annual catch of tuna was around 0.6 million tonnes;

▸ in 2010, it was about 6.6 million tonnes.

Today, most of the main tuna stocks have been exploited and very few remain undeveloped (FAO 2010). Over-fishing not only destroys marine ecosystems, it also pushes fishing villages into poverty as their means of earning a living are threatened – and a central element of their diet becomes increasingly rare.

The problem of by-catch

Two of the commercial methods of catching tuna include using large trawling nets and attracting schools of tuna with a "floating aggregation device" (FAD). The first method can lead to dolphins being caught in the net, because dolphins and tuna tend to swim together. As a result of many years of campaigning both at national and international level, it is now possible to find "dolphin-safe tuna".

The second method – the FAD – not only attracts tuna, but also many other species of marine life: for every 1 000 tonnes of yellowfin tuna caught using FAD, nearly 111 000 other creatures were caught – including turtles, sharks, rays and marlins (Forbes 2015). When eating a can of tuna, consumers are mostly unaware of the fact that it has probably led to a large number of other casualties.

Forced labour in the fishing industry

In order to keep canned tuna cheap, the fishing industry exploits vulnerable migrant workers to catch and process the seafood. According to Greenpeace, Thai Union, the biggest canned tuna company in the world, is associated with shocking labour rights abuses at sea. The Associated Press has documented the suffering of people who were trafficked and forced to work on fishing boats. Hlaing Min, a runaway slave from Benjina, told The Associated Press: "If Americans and Europeans are eating this fish, they should remember us. There must be a mountain of bones under the sea. ... The bones of the people could be an island, it's that many." (McDowell, Mason and Mendoza 2015).

Handout: fishing log

Fisher's name _____

After each season, record the numbers of target fish, by-catch and fish left in the ocean.

Part 1

Season	No. of goldfish left	No. of endangered species left	No. of other fish left
1			
2			
3			
4			
5			
6			

Part 2

Season	No. of goldfish left	No. of endangered species left	No. of other fish left
1			
2			
3			
4			
5			
6			

GREENWASHING

Overview

In this activity participants analyse advertisements to identify the false messaging at the heart of greenwashing. They use creative skills to develop their own awareness-raising advertisements against environmental threats.

Key concepts

Greenwashing, consumerism, environmental threats, sustainability, public relations

Complexity: Level 3

Group size: 4-30

Time: 90-120 minutes

Objectives

- ▶ to identify environmental threats caused by different industries;
- ▶ to understand the role of public relations (PR) and how it can be used to "greenwash" environmental threats;
- ▶ to develop critical thinking skills.

Materials

- ▶ some examples of greenwashing from www.greenwashingindex.com – or elsewhere. You can also use advertisements from newspapers or magazines: look for ones which boast about the good done to the environment;
- ▶ copies of the list of questions;
- ▶ paper and pens.

Preparation

Either print out a few examples from the website above, or arrange to project them onto a screen.

Instructions

1. Ask participants to brainstorm the most serious threats to the environment. Make a list of their suggestions down one side of a flip chart.

2. Now ask them to think of products or companies which contribute to these threats. Write these down the other side of the paper, and try to link the threat to the company.

You will probably find that many of the companies link to more than one of the threats.

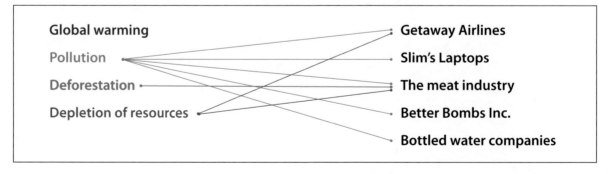

3. After about 10 minutes, or when you have filled a flip chart, ask participants how they know about the damage these companies do to the environment. Do they tell us?

4. Divide participants into groups of 4-5 people and give each group 2 examples of greenwashing advertisements and copies of the questions on page 51. Ask them to analyse the advertisements using the guiding questions. Give them about 10 minutes for this task.

5. When groups have finished answering the questions, ask for a quick show of hands to question 4 about whether the message in the advertisement was "true" about the product. Briefly ask groups about their answers to some of the other questions.

6. Explain the idea of greenwashing (see the definitions in the background information). You could also explain the idea of subvertising.

7. Hand out pieces of flip chart paper to the groups. Tell them to choose one of your products and create your own advertisement to "correct" the message put out by the producer. You want consumers to know what they are really buying with this product! Your advertisement could be a poster or short video for TV or radio (not more than 1 minute).

    Give them 20-30 minutes for this work.

8. Bring the group back together, and ask each small group to present its new advertisement.

Debriefing

Begin with brief feedback on the advertisements.

► What did you like about the advertisements created by one of the other groups?

► Do you think their message was more accurate than the company's own?

► Why is greenwashing a problem?

► Had you ever noticed examples of greenwashing before? Can you give any examples?

► What can be done about greenwashing? Who needs to do something about it? What could you do?

Tips for facilitators

The brainstorming in point 2 could also be done in small groups, and the suggestions could then be shared with other groups. This will take more time.

After the groups have worked on the questions, do not spend too much time discussing the answers. The purpose of these questions is for participants to begin analysing the advertisements, so they can create their own later.

You could check whether any organisations have engaged in subvertising company brands in your country – or whether there are international brands which have been subvertised and which ones participants will recognise. The sites www.adbusters.org and http://thesietch.org/mysietch/keith/subvertising-gallery offer some examples.

Suggestions for follow-up

The activity "A finite planet" looks at some of the hidden assumptions which guide mainstream thinking about consumerism and the need for growth. You could use this activity to inspect and then question some of the assumptions behind advertising slogans. You could also use "Waste manifesto", which looks at some of the effects of mass consumerism.

Ideas for action

Find out whether there is a body regulating advertisements in your country, and whether complaints relating to greenwashing – e.g. for misleading the public – can be submitted. Use the list you drew up in point 2, or build on it, to identify the worst offenders. Support participants to submit complaints – either to the regulating body or to the companies themselves.

Participants could also use their "subvertised" images to campaign against the companies. They could make them into placards or banners, or use them as memes on social media. This will raise awareness of the problem the company wished to hide through its greenwashing!

Background information – Greenwashing and subvertising

Definitions

It's greenwashing when a company or organization spends more time and money claiming to be "green" through advertising and marketing than actually implementing business practices that minimize environmental impact. It's whitewashing, but with a green brush (Greenwashing Index).

Greenwash: the phenomenon of socially and environmentally destructive corporations attempting to preserve and expand their markets by posing as friends of the environment and leaders in the struggle to eradicate poverty (CorpWatch 2001).

Greenwashing: when a company, government or other group promotes green-based environmental initiatives or images but actually operates in a way that is damaging to the environment or in an opposite manner to the goal of the announced initiatives. This can also include misleading customers about the environmental benefits of a product through misleading advertising and unsubstantiated claims (Investopedia).

Subvertising: is a portmanteau of subvert and advertise, and refers to the practice of making spoofs or parodies of corporate and political advertisements (Wikipedia).

Subvertising is an attempt to turn the iconography of the advertisers into a noose around their neck. If images can create a brand, they can also destroy one. A subvert is a satirical version or the defacing of an existing advert, a *detournement*, an inversion designed to make us forget consumerism and consider instead social or political issues (Barley 2001).

Handout: questions for groups

	Product 1	Product 2
1. What is the product being sold in this advert?		
2. What is it for, and why do people buy it?		
3. What message is the company trying to give consumers in this advertisement?		
4. Is the message really true about the product? Explain.		
5. Why do you think the company is trying to promote this message?		
6. Make a list of the most important effects on the environment of producing and selling this product.		

HOW BIG IS MY FOOT?

This activity is adapted from Turner (2004) and the Global Footprint Network.

Overview

Participants calculate their ecological footprint and explore changes they could make to their lifestyles to reduce their footprint.

Key concepts

Ecological footprint, Earth Overshoot Day, consumerism, waste, environmental threats

Complexity: Level 2

Group size: Any

Time: 60 minutes

Objectives

- ▶ to understand the dangers posed to the earth by human activity (Earth Overshoot Day);
- ▶ to appreciate the impact of our daily activities on the environment (ecological footprint);
- ▶ to identify ways of reducing the size of our personal footprint.

Materials

- ▶ ecological footprint quiz;
- ▶ pens and paper.

Preparation

- ▶ look through the quiz before carrying out the activity and review any questions which may be difficult to understand for your group of young people;
- ▶ print out the Ecological Footprint Calculator for each participant (see Handout).

Alternative: if your participants have access to the internet, you could use one of the online calculators, for example www.footprintcalculator.org or www.nature.org/greenliving/carboncalculator/index.htm.

Instructions

1. Ask participants if they have heard of Earth Overshoot Day. If they have not, invite them to share what they think it might mean.

2. Give them some information from the handout, and bring to their attention the fact that Earth Overshoot Day occurs earlier and earlier every year. This means that humans are depleting the earth's resources not just more and more, but more and more quickly.

3. Brainstorm some of the things which contribute to using up the ecological resources for a given year. Which actions that participants carry out in their daily lives are likely to contribute to the depletion of the earth's resources?

4. After the brainstorming, tell participants that we can make a rough calculation of our own contribution to this problem, using the Ecological Footprint Calculator. This is a questionnaire which assesses the amount of the earth's resources that we use as individuals.

5. Distribute the Ecological Footprint Calculator to all participants. Go through the first couple of questions so they understand how to arrive at a number for each question. Then invite them to work through the questionnaire individually, and arrive at a calculation for their footprint.

6. After participants finish, check the scores and discuss whether anyone is surprised by their own results, or those of others. Give participants some examples of average ecological footprints in different countries (see page 56). Ask for comments.

7. Explain that the average earth share is currently 1.9 hectares per person, and show participants how they can use their ecological footprint to calculate the number of planets which would be needed if everyone in the world used the same amount of resources.

To calculate the number of planets needed, divide your ecological footprint by the average earth share (1.9).

For example, suppose my footprint is 6.5.

$6.5 \div 1.9 = 3.4$

So 3.4 earths (planets) would be needed if everyone had the same footprint as me.

---

8. Ask participants to raise their hands:
   ▶ If less than one planet was needed;
   ▶ If between 1 and 2 planets were needed;
   ▶ If more than two planets were needed.

9. Ask for a few comments and reflections, then invite participants to spend a few minutes individually looking back at their questionnaire, reviewing their answers to different questions. Ask them all to identify up to three actions they could take to reduce their scores.

10. Give them 5-10 minutes for this then come back to the plenary to share participants' commitments to decrease their footprint.

Debriefing

Begin by asking participants to share their proposals for reducing their footprint, then use some of the questions below to debrief the activity.

▶ What were the three actions you came up with? How did you choose which areas of "overshoot" to address?

▶ Which of your daily practices or habits affected the score more? Can you address any of these?

▶ Do you think you will carry out the actions you identified (or those identified by someone else)?

▶ What might make it difficult to carry them out, and how could you overcome this difficulty?

▶ What are the consequences of not changing some of our routine practices? Who – or what – are the "victims" of overshooting the planet's resources?

▶ Who has responsibility for making sure we preserve the earth's resources? Is it enough for individuals to change their habits?

▶ What can we do to preserve the earth's resources not only through our personal actions, but also at the national or international level?

Tips for facilitators

If it is possible for participants to carry out the online questionnaire, this will not only be easier for you to prepare, it will also be better for the environment!

The comparison between countries and regions is important. However, try not to lead the discussion as if only citizens from countries with the biggest footprints are solely responsible to act. You can find country footprints at www.footprintnetwork.org/resources/data.

You can learn more about ecological footprints at wwf.panda.org/about_our_earth/all_publications/lpr_2016/ and about Earth Overshoot Day at www.footprintnetwork.org/our-work/earth-overshoot-day/.

Suggestions for follow-up

The activity "Needs and wants" stimulates discussion on the things we really need, and those we think we need – or those that society makes us believe we need! This might be a good follow-up for participants as it will lead them to question some of the choices they make in their lives, and the impact this might have on the environment.

Alternatively, "Chicken sandwich" looks at the threats to our environment as a result of the food choices we make.

Ideas for action

Participants can continue to calculate their footprint at regular intervals, and try to decrease it by taking some of the actions they have identified.

They could try to find out if their school or local municipality would be interested in addressing their ecological footprint. Alternatively, encourage them to think about joining or starting a campaign for more investment into cycling routes and public transport in the city.

Participants could also develop and run an awareness-raising campaign on Earth Overshoot Day.

Background information – Ecological footprint

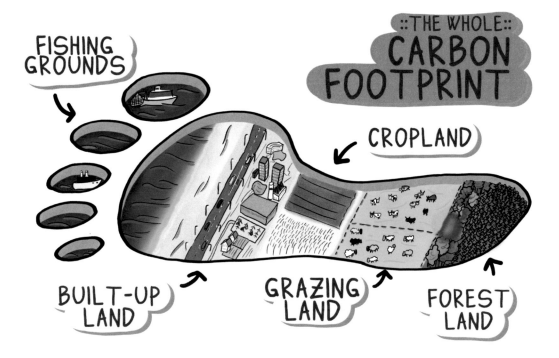

In the 1990s, the term "ecological footprint" was coined to refer to the load or demand that we place on the earth's resources. An ecological footprint is a measure of how much of the earth's biologically productive land and water is needed to produce our food, material goods and energy, and to absorb our waste.

The earth has a total surface area of 51 billion hectares, but less than one quarter of this – under 12 billion hectares – is biologically productive for human use. In Figure 10, this is represented by the green and blue areas. The amount of land available on the planet to provide all of the food, water and other materials that we need to support ourselves is therefore 12 billion hectares.

Figure 10. The earth's surface and its productive land

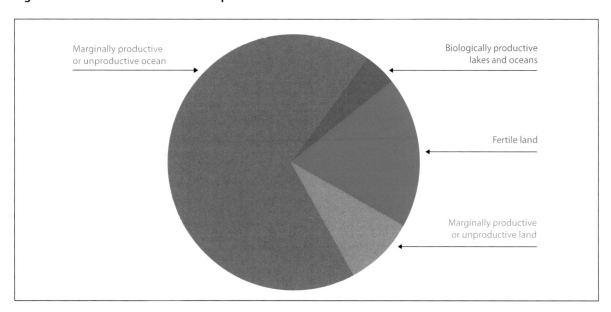

The human population in 2017 was about 7.6 billion, and climbing. Of the biologically productive land and water that is available, our average earth share is 1.6 hectares per person (12 billion/7.6 billion). This is the maximum amount of the earth's surface, for the present population, that the earth can sustain without our slowly depleting the resources available.

The footprint of the "average" person differs from country to country:

- Luxembourg: 15.8 hectares/person;
- United States: 8.2 hectares/person;
- United Kingdom: 7.9 hectares/person;
- Russian Federation: 5.7 hectares/person;
- Italy: 4.6 hectares/person;
- Serbia: 2.7 hectares/person;
- Afghanistan: 0.8 hectares/person;
- Eritrea: 0.4 hectares/person.

Note that the average footprint in most of the listed countries is greater than what the earth can sustain.

Earth Overshoot Day

Earth Overshoot Day marks the date when the world uses up all of the ecological resources available for a given year and starts living on resources borrowed from future generations. It shows the gap between our demands on the earth and how much it is able to provide.

As humans, we have always made use of nature's resources. However, beginning in 1970, our consumption first began to outstrip what the earth was able to reproduce. Since then, humans have used up more than the earth can sustain with increasing rapidity. As year follows year, the earth's natural resources have become increasingly depleted.

Today, on average, humans demand the equivalent of more than 1.5 earths every year. It is estimated that before the middle of this century, this may increase to two earths every year.

Earth Overshoot dates

- 1970: December 31
- 1987: December 19
- 1990: December 7
- 1995: November 21
- 2000: November 1
- 2005: October 20
- 2008: September 23
- 2010: August 21
- 2014: August 19
- 2015: August 13
- 2016: August 8
- 2017: August 2

Handout: my Ecological Footprint Calculator

Write down the number in brackets corresponding to your answer: e.g. if your shower normally lasts between 3 and 6 minutes, write 70 in the blank space.

My score   **My score**

Water use

1. My shower on a typical day is:
   - ▶ No shower (0)
   - ▶ 1-2 minutes long (50)
   - ▶ 3-6 minutes long (70)
   - ▶ 10 or more minutes long (90)

2. I flush the toilet:
   - ▶ Every time I use it (40)
   - ▶ Sometimes (20)

3. When I brush my teeth, I let the water run.
   - ▶ Yes (40)
   - ▶ No (0)

4. I washed the car or watered the lawn today.
   - ▶ Yes (80)
   - ▶ No (0)

5. We use water-saving toilets (6-9 litres/flush).
   - ▶ Yes (-20)
   - ▶ No (0)

6. We use low-flow showerheads.
   - ▶ Yes (-20)
   - ▶ No (0)

7. I use a dishwasher on a typical day.
   - ▶ Yes (50)
   - ▶ No (0)

Water use subtotal:

Food

1. On a typical day, I eat:
   Select any that apply
   - ▶ Beef (150/portion)
   - ▶ Chicken (100/portion)
   - ▶ Farmed fish (80/portion)
   - ▶ Wild fish (40/portion)
   - ▶ Eggs (40/portion)
   - ▶ Milk/dairy (40/portion)
   - ▶ Fruit (20/portion)
   - ▶ Vegetables (20/portion)
   - ▶ Grains: bread, cereal, rice (20/portion)

2. ____ of my food is grown locally.
   - ▶ All (0)
   - ▶ Some (30)
   - ▶ None (60)

3. ____ of my food is organic.
   - ▶ All (0)
   - ▶ Some (30)
   - ▶ None (60)

4. I compost my fruit/vegetable scraps and peels.
   - ▶ Yes (-20)
   - ▶ No (60)

5. ____ of my food is processed.
   - ▶ All (100)
   - ▶ Some (30)
   - ▶ None (0)

6. ____ of my food has packaging.
   - ▶ All (100)
   - ▶ Some (30)
   - ▶ Nonc (0)

7. On a typical day, I waste:
   - ▶ None of my food (0)
   - ▶ One fourth of my food (100)
   - ▶ One third of my food (150)
   - ▶ Half of my food (200)

Food subtotal:

Transportation

1. On a typical day, I travel by:
   - Foot (0)
   - Bike (5 per use)
   - Public transport (30 per use)
   - Private vehicle (200 per use)

2. Our vehicle's fuel efficiency is
   ____ litres/100 kilometres.
   - less than 6 litres (-50)
   - 6-9 litres (50)
   - 10-13 litres (100)
   - More than 13 litres (200)

3. The time I spend in vehicles
   on a typical day is:
   - No time (0)
   - Less than half an hour (40)
   - Half an hour to 1 hour (60)
   - More than 1 hour (100)

4. How big is the car in which
   I travel on a typical day?
   - No car (-20)
   - Small (50)
   - Medium (100)
   - Large (SUV) (200)

5. How many cars are there
   in our driveway?
   - No car (-20)
   - 1 car (50)
   - 2 cars (100)
   - More than 2 cars (200)

6. On a typical day, I walk/run for:
   - 5 hours or more (-75)
   - 3 to 5 hours (-25)
   - 1 to 3 hours (0)
   - Half an hour to 1 hour (10)
   - Less than 10 minutes (100)

Transportation subtotal:

Shelter

1. Number of rooms per person
   (divide number of rooms by
   number of people living at home)
   - Fewer than 2 rooms per person (10)
   - 2 to 3 rooms per person (80)
   - 4 to 6 rooms per person (140)
   - 7 or more rooms per person (200)

2. We share our home with
   non-family members.
   - Yes (-50)
   - No (0)

3. We own a second, or holiday
   home that is often empty.
   - No (0)
   - We own/use it with others (200)
   - Yes (400)

Shelter subtotal:

Energy use

1. In cold months,
   our house temperature is:
   - Under 15° C (-20)
   - 15-18° C (50)
   - 19-22° C (100)
   - 22° C or more (150)

2. We dry clothes outdoors
   or on an indoor rack.
   - Always (-50)
   - Sometimes (20)
   - Never (60)

3. We use an energy-efficient refrigerator. ☐
   ▸ Yes (-50)
   ▸ No (50)

4. We use compact fluorescent light bulbs. ☐
   ▸ Yes (-50)
   ▸ No (50)

5. I turn off lights, computer and
   television when they are not in use. ☐
   ▸ Yes (0)
   ▸ No (50)

6. To cool off, I use: ☐
   ▸ Air conditioning:
     car/home (30 for each)
   ▸ Electric fan (-10)
   ▸ Nothing (-50)

7. Outdoors today, I spent: ☐
   ▸ 7 hours (0)
   ▸ 4 to 6 hours (10)
   ▸ 2 to 3 hours (20)
   ▸ 2 hours or less (100)

Energy use subtotal: ☐

Clothing

1. I change my outfit every day
   and put it in the laundry. ☐
   ▸ Yes (80)
   ▸ No (0)

2. I am wearing clothes that have
   been mended or fixed. ☐
   ▸ Yes (-20)
   ▸ No (0)

3. One fourth of my clothes are
   handmade or second-hand. ☐
   ▸ Yes (-20)
   ▸ No (0)

4. Most of my clothes are
   purchased new each year. ☐
   ▸ Yes (120)
   ▸ No (0)

5. I give the local charity shop
   clothes that I no longer wear. ☐
   ▸ Yes (0)
   ▸ No (100)

6. I buy hemp instead of
   cotton shirts when I can. ☐
   ▸ Yes (-10)
   ▸ No (0)

7. I never wear ___ %
   of the clothes in my cupboard. ☐
   ▸ Less than 25% (25)
   ▸ 50% (50)
   ▸ 75% (75)
   ▸ More than 75% (100)

8. I have _____ pairs of shoes. ☐
   ▸ 2 to 3 (20)
   ▸ 4 to 6 (60)
   ▸ 7 or more (90)

Clothing subtotal: ☐

Stuff

1. All my rubbish from today
   could fit into a: ☐
   ▸ Shoebox (20)
   ▸ Large bucket (60)
   ▸ Garbage can (200)
   ▸ No rubbish created today! (-50)

2. I reuse items rather than throw
   them out. ☐
   ▸ Yes (-20)
   ▸ No (0)

3. I repair items rather than
   throw them out. ☐
   ▸ Yes (-20)
   ▸ No (0)

4. I recycle all my paper, cans, glass and plastic.

▸ Yes (-20)

▸ No (0)

6. I use rechargeable batteries whenever I can.

▸ Yes (-30)

▸ No (0)

5. I avoid disposable items as often as possible.

▸ Yes (-10)

▸ No (60)

7. Add one point for each euro you spend in a typical day.

Today was a Buy Nothing Day (0)
Outdoors today, I spent:

Stuff subtotal:

Fun

1. In my locality, the land converted into fields, rinks, pools, gyms, ski slopes, car parks, etc. added together occupy:

▸ Nothing (0)

▸ Less than 1 hectare (20)

▸ 1 to 2 hectares (60)

▸ 2 or more hectares (100)

3. How much equipment is needed for typical activities?

▸ None (0)

▸ Very little (20)

▸ Some (60)

▸ A lot (80)

Fun subtotal:

2. On a typical day, I use the TV or computer:

▸ Not at all (0)

▸ Less than 1 hour (50)

▸ More than 1 hour (80)

Summary

Transfer your subtotals from each section and add them together to obtain the grand total.

▸ Energy use

▸ Water use

▸ Clothing

▸ Food

▸ Stuff

▸ Transportation

▸ Fun

▸ Shelter

Grand total:

My ecological footprint is:

Grand total divided by 100 = _____ hectares

MAPPING THE GLOBE

Overview

The activity uses mind-mapping to point up the connections between human rights and the environment.

Key concepts

Health, food, water, human rights

Complexity: Level 3

Group size: 9-20

Time: 90 minutes

Objectives

▶ to understand the close connection between environmental questions and human rights;

▶ to explore the meaning of the rights to health, food and water;

▶ to develop skills of co-operation and analysis.

Materials

▶ flip chart paper;

▶ masking tape or Blu-Tack;

▶ Post-its or a few additional blank cards for each group;

▶ coloured pens.

Preparation

▶ make copies of the cards on page 65 and cut them out. Each group will need a set of cards (there are three groups altogether);

▶ prepare a large sheet of paper for each group: this could be 2 pieces of flip chart paper taped down the middle. In the centre of each group's sheet, write one of the following:

  – right to health;

  – right to water;

  – right to food.

▶ make sure you have enough room for 3 groups to work around their sheet of paper.

Instructions

1. Ask participants what they know about the rights to health, food and water. Provide them with basic information from the background information "Human rights and environmental protection" if they cannot supply it themselves.

2. Explain that the activity will explore the connection between these human rights and environmental protection, using the process of a mind map. Provide an example of a mind map if participants have not used this method before.

3. Divide participants into three groups, and allocate one of the rights to health, food or water to each group. Give each group the flip chart paper you have prepared and a set of cards.

4. Tell groups that they have 45 minutes to produce a mind map connecting as many of the key terms as they can. Explain that if the connections are not obvious, they will need to provide information within their diagram – for example in the connecting links between two cards. They may also wish to include more key terms of their own. Provide them with some additional blank pieces of paper or sticky notes in case they wish to do this.

5.	After 40 minutes, invite the groups to look at the mind maps produced by other groups. Ask them to make a note of anything that is not clear or where they need further information from the group responsible.

6.	Bring all participants back together for the debriefing.

Debriefing

▸ How did you find the task – was it easy, difficult, enjoyable?

▸ Did you manage to include all the key words in your map? Could you have done so with more time?

▸ How easy was it to identify the links? Which ones were least obvious?

▸ Was the task helpful in terms of clarifying concepts or in terms of seeing connections?

▸ Did you learn anything new from anyone in your group?

▸ What did you notice about the maps produced by other groups? Did you have any questions?

▸ What are the main conclusions you would draw from the discussions you had?

▸ Do you think it makes sense to talk about the right to environmental protection?

▸ Do you notice examples of the environment affecting people's rights in your society?

▸ How can you help to protect the environment in your everyday life?

▸ Do you think that young people are conscious enough of the links between environmental protection and human rights? Can you think of ways to make these links more explicit?

Tips for facilitators

The activity includes some terms that you may need to familiarise yourself with before introducing them to participants. If you think participants may be unfamiliar with some of the terms, you could miss out some cards, or replace them with terms participants will know. Alternatively, allow them to look things up as they work.

It is important for you to familiarise yourself with the mind-mapping tool: look at the example provided below (Figure 11) and make sure you feel confident about explaining it to participants. It is always useful to work on a few branches with participants before asking them to do their own maps.

When they draw their own maps, encourage them to be creative and include details or visual aids such as icons, drawings, arrows, highlighting or other methods.

When the groups have finished their maps you could simply invite them to walk around and look at the maps of other groups. If groups want to present their results they should be advised to talk briefly about the process, perhaps focusing on difficulties or points of disagreement, rather than trying to talk through the map itself.

You can find brief information below concerning the specific human rights that groups will be working on.

Suggestions for follow-up

The activity "The cost of fashion" looks at human rights and sustainability issues connected to the textile industry.

You could also use the activity "Our futures" for participants to begin thinking about a holistic response to some of the sustainability issues in their community.

Ideas for action

Draw up a list of concrete ways in which they can help to protect the environment. Help them put it into practice!

Background information – Human rights and environmental protection

The rights to health, food and water

Everyone has the right to a standard of living adequate for the health and well-being of himself and of his family.

(Article 25, Universal Declaration of Human Rights)

The States Parties to the present Covenant recognize the right of everyone to an adequate standard of living for himself and his family, including adequate food … The States Parties will take appropriate steps to ensure the realization of this right, recognizing to this effect the essential importance of international co-operation based on free consent.

(Article 11, International Covenant on Economic, Social and Cultural Rights)

The States Parties to the present Covenant recognize the right of everyone to the enjoyment of the highest attainable standard of physical and mental health.

(Article 12, International Covenant on Economic, Social and Cultural Rights)

The right to health was recognised as early as 1946, when the constitution of the World Health Organization (WHO) stated that the enjoyment of the highest attainable standard of health is one of the fundamental rights of every human being.

In 2000, the United Nations Committee on Economic, Social and Cultural Rights, the Covenant's supervisory body, adopted a General Comment on the right to health that provides an interpretation of the right to health as enshrined in Article 12 of the Covenant. This General Comment interprets the right to health as an inclusive right that extends not only to timely and appropriate health care but also to those factors that determine good health. These include access to safe drinking water and adequate sanitation, a sufficient supply of safe food, nutrition and housing, healthy occupational and environmental conditions, and access to health-related education and information.

In 2002, the UN Committee further recognised that water itself was an independent right. Drawing on a range of international treaties and declarations, it stated that "the right to water clearly falls within the category of guarantees essential for securing an adequate standard of living, particularly since it is one of the most fundamental conditions for survival".

Human rights and the right to environmental protection

In parts of Europe, as in all other parts of the world, there are people facing acute water shortages, declining fish supplies, deforestation, pollution and other environmental disasters. The victims of these disasters are not just animals and wildlife, they include humans as well. More often than not, the humans who are affected are those least able to defend themselves: the poor, the disadvantaged, the marginalised.

The issues of human rights and environmental protection come together in a world that manages to protect and nurture both human and non-human life in a sustainable way. It is increasingly obvious that the questions of environmental degradation and human rights violations are heavily interdependent and an understanding of the common issues can only help our efforts to work for each of them.

For further information on the links between environmental rights and the European Convention on Human Rights, see "Environmental protection and the European Convention on Human Rights", available at www.echr.coe.int/LibraryDocs/DG2/HRFILES/DG2-EN-HRFILES-21(2005).pdf. Also see the Declaration on the United Nations Conference on the Human Environment (Stockholm Declaration), available at www.un-documents.net/unchedec.htm.

Background information – Mind-mapping

Mind-mapping is a simple and powerful tool, a non-linear way of organising information and a technique that allows the natural flow of ideas to be captured. The purpose is to cluster similar ideas, to see links between them and to pick out the most important issues, particularly when discussing or brainstorming. It is a good way of making sure that all aspects of a situation have been considered. Start with the central issue or question and build outwards like a tree, extending branches to make sub-branches and even sub-sub-branches. You should end up with a spider's web of interconnected concepts.

For further information on mind-mapping see: https://thinksmart.com.

Figure 11. Example of mind-mapping

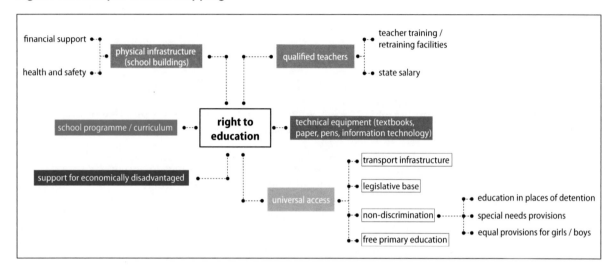

Handout: key words

environmental protection	human rights	agricultural productivity	children's health	coastal systems	diet
economic development	social development	cultural development	food distribution	adequate food	healthy development of the child
infant mortality	land occupations	nutrition	food resources	arable land	crops
irrigation	dams	immigration	minority	soil depletion	food and agriculture policies
food safety	pesticides	food security	wetlands	estuaries	fisheries
globalisation	refugees	labour issues	rural development	trade	sustainable development
urbanisation	pesticides	disease	drugs	climate change	natural hazards
local knowledge	pollution	waste	watersheds	rivers	nuclear energy
marine mammals	groundwater	peace	conflict	forest	deforestation
toxins	biodiversity	cultural diversity	Europe	Mediterranean	culture
right to property	right to health	right to food	NGO	youth organisations	

NATURE JOURNALISTS

Overview

This is an outdoor activity that aims to recreate a sense of connection with nature and the environment.

Key concepts

Nature and the environment, biodiversity

Complexity: Level 1

Group size: Any

Time: 60 minutes

Objectives

- ▶ to develop a sense of connection to nature;
- ▶ to motivate young people to spend more time in nature;
- ▶ to develop skills of observation.

Materials

- ▶ a sheet of A4 paper and a pen for each participant;
- ▶ (optional) photo cameras or other devices that can take photos.

Preparation

Find a calm spot in nature. It can be a nearby forest, urban park or garden. If possible, take participants out of the city/town: their experiences will be stronger the further they are from urban life.

Instructions

1. Inform participants that today they will be nature journalists, and will explore a natural site. Give each participant a sheet of A4 paper and a pen.

    Optional: if a camera or smartphone is available for every participant, you could allow them to use these. Do not allow cameras/smartphones if some participants do not have access to them.

2. Once you are at the site, prepare participants for the experience by reminding them that nature is a great place to get rid of stress, or to breathe cleaner air than in a city, or to find peace and quiet. Tell them that they have about 30 minutes to explore nature, without talking to each other. They can take notes (and photos) in these 30 minutes, on the following signs of life:
    - signs of dependence (one thing being dependent on another);
    - signs of change;
    - signs of human activity;
    - something unusual or surprising;
    - an animal, a vegetable and a mineral;
    - biodiversity (the wide variety of living things);
    - their feelings.

3. After 30 minutes, bring them back together and ask them to share their notes in small groups (3-5 participants).

4. Bring the whole group together for a debriefing after a further 15-20 minutes.

Debriefing

Begin by asking for answers to a few of the questions they investigated. You could ask participants to share not their own answers, but the answers of others in their small group. Then discuss some of the following questions.

> ▸ Did you enjoy the experience outside? What did you like or not like?

> ▸ Did you discover anything new or unexpected?

> ▸ Did your answers differ from those of others in your small group? Can you explain this?

> ▸ Many natural sites risk disappearing because of human activity, such as industry, agriculture, or pollution. Did anyone find any evidence of this?

> ▸ Did spending some time in nature remind you of the value of the environment?

> ▸ What role does nature play in the survival of humanity, and the planet as a whole?

> ▸ How can we make sure that nature and the environment are better defended?

Tips for facilitators

If your group is small, you could bring participants straight back together for the debriefing.

Depending on the group of young people you work with, you may wish to have a thematic exploration of nature. For example, you could ask participants to identify as many species of trees or plants as they can in 30 minutes, and then have a discussion on the value of biodiversity.

Suggestions for follow-up

The activity "Waste manifesto" looks at the effects of pollution on the natural environment, beginning with an investigation of participants' own habits of throwing things away.

You could also try the activity "Take a step forward" in which participants role play people in other parts of the globe, often severely disadvantaged by the environmental effects of human activity.

Ideas for action

Try to find out more about who is responsible for looking after the natural site where you ran your activity – if anyone is. Are there any mechanisms in place to safeguard the biodiversity? Are there any possible threats to the site?

If participants are interested, you could explore ways of creating a small garden together – perhaps taking on an allotment, or looking around for unused land that could be developed. Take a look at www.guerrillagardening.org for inspiration!

NEEDS AND WANTS

Overview

This activity looks at the difference between needs and wants, how we define each, and why this matters for the planet's sustainability.

Key concepts

Health, planning, local environment, development, community

Complexity: Level 1

Group size: Any

Time: 45 minutes

Objectives

▶ to understand the difference between needs and wants;
▶ to appreciate the relationship between consumption and sustainability;
▶ to be able to identify ways to reduce our environmental impact.

Materials

▶ "Needs and wants" cards

Preparation

▶ Make copies of the cards and cut out the cards. You will need 1 set per pair or small group. Put each set into an envelope.

Instructions

1. Ask participants to pair up or work in small groups. Hand out a set of "needs and wants" cards to each group.

2. Tell groups to open their envelopes, and take 5 minutes to divide the set of cards into two piles:
    – things you need to live a healthy life (needs);
    – things you do not necessarily need, but that might be nice to have (wants).

3. After about 15 minutes, ask participants to comment on their choices. You could draw up a general list on a flip chart to reflect the choices of the group. Use the left- and right-hand column to put needs or wants where there is no disagreement.

Agreed needs	Possible needs/possible wants	Agreed wants

Briefly discuss the following questions:

- which cards were difficult to classify as either needs or wants? Why?
- was there any disagreement in your group over how to classify cards?
- which cards were definitely needs, and which were definitely wants?

4. After a short discussion, ask participants to go back into their groups and shuffle the cards again. This time they should divide them into piles:

- things that end up being thrown away or wasted (at least in part);
- things that are not thrown away or wasted.

5. Give them about 5 minutes to complete the task then debrief the whole activity.

Debriefing

Use a few of the questions from either section to debrief the activity.

Needs and wants

▶ What is the difference between a "need" and a "want"?
▶ How did you differentiate between your wants and needs? Was it easy?
▶ Why do you think there was disagreement about how to classify the cards as needs or wants?
▶ How do you feel when your needs are not fulfilled? How do you feel when your wants are not fulfilled? What is the difference?
▶ Do you think your needs would have been different if you had lived 200 years ago?
▶ Are there people in the world who don't have their basic needs met? What about people in your community?
▶ Is there anything in the "want" column which is actually necessary for human existence – even If you didn't think it was a need for you?
▶ Use this question as an opportunity to speak about the role that trees, flowers, insects, etc. play in sustaining life on earth.

Waste

▶ How easy did you find this part? What was difficult?
▶ Do you think we "throw away" some of the things nature provides – e.g. sunlight, water, trees? How could we make better use of these things (and why does it matter)?
▶ Do you ever recycle your own possessions? Do you ever use recycled possessions from other people?
▶ The earth is huge: does it really matter if we throw things away or do not recycle properly?

Suggestions for follow-up

You could follow up with the activity "Waste manifesto", which looks at how much participants throw away and helps to develop a policy for the group on waste.

The activity "Nature journalists" takes participants out into nature in order for them to reconnect, and see the importance of preserving a healthy environment.

Ideas for action

Find out if Buy Nothing Day is held in your country, or select your own date when the group will agree to buy nothing, and publicise this in the local community. Support them to create placards and information leaflets to hand out in advance of the day.

Handout: "needs and wants" cards

Security	Love	Being able to walk	Internet
Friends	Being able to talk	Trees	Meat
Insects	Jokes	Freedom	Bicycle
TV	Cellphone/ Smartphone	Laptop	Car
Fruit	Family	Birds	Bees
Sunlight	Water	Rain	Soil
Money	Bed	Flowers	Books
Entertainment	Food	Clothes	Electricity
Medicine	Radio	Theatre	Air
Toys	Shoes	Music	Soap
Paper	Heat	Vegetables	Home

NEOCLEAR INC.

Overview

This is a simulation exercise exploring different opinions on nuclear energy and sustainability.

Key concepts

Energy sources, nuclear energy, nuclear waste, renewable energy, sustainability

Complexity: Level 4

Group size: 10-20

Time: 120 minutes

Objectives

▶ to explore social, economic and environmental concerns relating to nuclear energy;

▶ to negotiate conflict arising from different needs and visions of society;

▶ to explore energy transitions and their costs and impact on society;

▶ to develop debating and analytical skills.

Materials

▶ a large space that can be arranged as a municipal hall for a public hearing, with the possibility of separate spaces for work in small groups;

▶ copies of role cards and sheets of paper for name tags;

▶ a watch or clock;

▶ a small bell for the Mayor of Floville;

▶ paper and pens.

Preparation

▶ photocopy the role cards in the handout, the description of the problem and the rules of debate (optional). You will need a copy of the Mayor's role card and equal numbers of representatives in the different groups (as far as possible);

▶ prepare name tags for the different parties/groups that will be represented at the meeting;

▶ list the different roles on a flip chart so that everyone can see them;

▶ make sure you have space for the Town Council Meeting and separate spaces for the different groups, so that they can discuss their position beforehand or meet with others.

Instructions

1. Read out the description of the problem. Explain that all participants (except the representatives of the Windland Parliament) are citizens of Floville and are troubled by the problem of whether the nuclear plant not far from the city should close down.

2. Show participants the list of different roles and ask everyone to select one. Hand out the role cards and the description of the problem and indicate where people and groups can meet up beforehand, and where the Town Council Meeting will take place later on.

3. Explain the rules of debate that will be used during the meeting. If possible, display these in a prominent place.

4. Explain that there will be 30 minutes before the actual meeting so that people can meet other citizens, prepare what they want to say and decide how they want to vote. Tell them that the Town Council Meeting will last 40 minutes, and that there may be very little time for actual speeches because

of the number of people attending. For that reason, they should try to prepare just 1 or 2 points that they want to make.

5. Use the preparation phase to set up the space for the council meeting. Ideally, people should sit in a semi-circle or horseshoe shape, with the Mayor at the front, in a slightly elevated position. Parties or groups should be able to sit together, and you should place their name tags on the tables in front.

6. After 30 minutes, call the citizens for the meeting (or ask the Mayor to do so). He/she should remind people of the basic rules of debate and give a short speech to introduce the meeting.

7. At the end of the meeting, after 40 minutes, the Mayor should call for a vote. When the votes have been counted and the result declared, announce the end of the activity, and invite people to bring their chairs into a circle for the debriefing.

Debriefing

Start the feedback by greeting everybody by their real names, or use another technique to enable participants to give up the roles they had during the simulation. This is important before starting the debriefing.

Gather some feelings from participants about the process, before going on to discuss issues raised by the activity.

- ▶ Were you surprised by the result of the vote, and did it reflect the position of the person you were playing?
- ▶ Did interaction with other people or groups make you alter your approach or your attitude towards the problem?
- ▶ What were the most persuasive arguments for you?
- ▶ How easy was it to identify with your role? Why or why not?
- ▶ Do you think that this role play was realistic? Could a similar case happen in your community? Can you think of examples where it has?
- ▶ How would you react if there was a proposal to build a nuclear energy plant in your town/place of residence? Did the activity alter your attitude at all?
- ▶ What do you understand by living in a clean environment, or living in a sustainable world?
- ▶ What can we all do to reduce the amount of energy we use, or to influence the sources of energy?

Tips for facilitators

If possible, you should run this activity with a co-facilitator in order to be able to answer questions and co-ordinate each step of the activity at the same time. The activity could also benefit from having more time available, particularly during the actual meeting, so that participants have the chance to respond to comments made by others.

During the preparation phase, it may be useful to check that participants are using the time to meet others or to plan what they are going to say during the meeting.

You could allocate the roles beforehand or distribute them randomly in order to save time during the session. Note that the role of the Mayor is a very demanding one, and the person playing it will need to feel confident about facilitating the meeting and – if necessary – cutting people short in order to allow everyone to speak.

You may need to go through the task with the participant playing the role of Mayor before the actual simulation. However, during the simulation, you should try to play no active role, both in order that the person playing the Mayor feels trusted by you, and in order that other participants respect his/her decisions rather than looking to you. Of course, if difficulties arise, you may find it necessary to intervene in the course of the simulation, but you should try to do this without undermining the authority of the participant playing the Mayor.

If the simulation gets out of control – for example, because people stray off the topic or new pieces of information are invented – or if the council gets caught in a deadlock and cannot come to an agreement, point out that this can reflect a result in real life, and does not indicate that the activity has failed. You can use this in the debriefing at the end to discuss the difficulty of reaching agreement on issues such as these.

During the debriefing, it is very important to try to avoid repeating the simulation. People need to try to detach themselves from the role they played in the activity in order to be able to reflect properly on what they have been through. You should help them to look back on the simulation with their normal "hats" on rather than in their assumed roles.

Depending on the context you are working in, it may be more appropriate to build the activity around questions of energy coming from fossil fuels or coal, for example. Or you may prefer some other combination. You can add news reporters to the activity in order to get a view on the process which is slightly detached; this, however, can add to the time, if you want to discuss the reports with the group (see below for suggestions).

Suggestions for follow-up

You could follow up the activity by looking at the impact of carbon-based energy sources on the environment. The activities "Chain reactions" and "Climate superhero auditions" address this issue.

You could also encourage participants to further explore the arguments for and against nuclear energy. The following websites, among many others, offer some arguments:

www.debatingeurope.eu/focus/infobox-arguments-for-and-against-nuclear/#.Wo1yXXxG1aR

http://100-gute-gruende.de/pdf/g100rs_en.pdf (based on the German context)

Ideas for action

Participants could research the energy companies working in the area to see whether they use any of the main renewable energy sources: wind, solar, biomass, hydro or geothermal. They could draw up a comparison, taking account of any plans by these companies to move away from carbon-based fuels (like coal, oil or gas).

Encourage participants to let the "dirtiest" energy companies know that, as potential customers, they are deeply concerned about the impact of their companies on the environment. There may even be local organisations or initiatives which they could join in campaigning for cleaner energy.

Depending on the context where you and the participants live or work and the current issues being debated within the town councils, it may be interesting to visit a council meeting in your area in order to see how these work in practice.

Resources for the debate

List of participants in the meeting

Try to keep the numbers balanced by having the same number of representatives for each political party, and the same number in each of the citizens' groups. You can have as many ordinary citizens as you like.

Role	No of participants
The Mayor of Floville	1
Town Council Members: 3 different parties should be represented. Try to make the parties equal in size	3-6
Trade union representing the workers at the plant	1-2
Stop Nuclear Energy group	1-2
EF – Energy for the Future	1-2
Representatives of the Windland Parliament	1-2
Ordinary citizens	Any
Optional: journalists who will report on the meeting	1-2

Rules of debate

You may wish to alter these rules according to the size of your group and the time you have available:

- ▸ the meeting will be chaired by the Mayor, and his/her decision on all matters is final;
- ▸ if you wish to speak, you should raise your hand and obtain permission from the Mayor;
- ▸ comments should be brief, and should not exceed 2 minutes;
- ▸ the meeting will close after 40 minutes, with a vote on whether or not the nuclear plant should be closed down;
- ▸ anyone attending the meeting is entitled to speak and to vote at the end.

Scenario

Will NeoClear close down?

You live in the picturesque town of Floville, a town of about 70 000 people. Your town is perhaps best known for its nuclear plant, NeoClear, which was built 30 years ago. Over 2 000 people in your town and the surrounding areas are employed either directly or indirectly by this nuclear plant. This has been of benefit not just to those individuals, but also to the local economy.

However, NeoClear is an older model of nuclear plant, and a number of recent independent assessments have questioned its safety. Since NeoClear's very beginnings, it has seen protests from groups and citizens, but these recent studies have escalated the protests and calls have been heard for it to be closed down completely.

The area around NeoClear carries a low risk of earthquakes and the plant is also built on top of a large aquifer. When it was first built, the company assured its critics that methods had been put in place to remove the risk of radiation polluting the water supply. Not everyone believed it. More recently, partly because of the tragic events at Fukushima in 2011, but also for other reasons such as the risk of terrorism and the age of the nuclear plant, local politicians have called for the plant to be closed down. There has even been international pressure: NeoClear is not far from the international border with neighbouring Windland, whose parliament has already voted to stop using nuclear energy.

The people of Floville cannot decide to close down NeoClear on their own, but they can take a popular vote which will have to be taken into account by national decision makers. The Town Council has called for a special meeting, to which all are invited, to resolve this issue.

The meeting will take place in 30 minutes.

Handout: role cards

The Mayor of Floville

You are chairing the meeting and it will be your role, once it begins, to welcome the participants and remind them of the rules of debate. During the meeting, you should try to give everyone the opportunity to speak – and should not allow anyone to speak for too long!

You are very worried about the bad publicity that this case has been attracting and you plan to try, before the meeting, to speak to some of the groups to try to persuade them to soften their positions.

Town Council Member: Republican Party

You represent the Republican Party on the Town Council. You generally support any forms of energy which can reduce the costs for the state and ensure as much tax revenue as possible. You believe that nuclear energy offers a good alternative to dirty fossil fuels like oil, coal and natural gas. Nuclear energy seems like the perfect solution for the future, as it pollutes less and is cheaper (in the short term).

You are also aware of the number of people working at the nuclear plant who will be out of work if it is closed down. You do not want to alienate potential voters.

Town Council Member: Populist Party

You represent the Populist Party on the Town Council. You stand for the people, and you are worried about the number of people who will lose their jobs if the nuclear plant closes down. You are inclined to support keeping the plant open, but you are also concerned about the health, environmental and safety risks.

You are aware that your seat is under threat at the next council elections, so you will probably support whichever option appears to be more popular.

Town Council Member: Green Party

You represent the Green Party on the Town Council. You believe it was a mistake to open this plant in the first place and you want it closed as soon as possible. The Fukushima disaster showed the world what your party has always said: we need green and renewable energies, and nuclear energy is neither of these. It is unsafe, and is more expensive than others if costs such as health risks, waste disposal and security costs – for example against terrorist attacks – are all taken into account. The cost of storing nuclear waste is enormous, and there is no technology today which allows us to do so safely. Green alternatives are possible, and our neighbours from Windland have shown us that this is a good political solution. Workers can easily be reintegrated from the old nuclear plant into renewable energies – so the jobs of 2 000 people are not at risk!

Members of the trade union representing the workers at the plant

You represent the workers at the NeoClear plant. This plant helps over 2 000 people earn a living, in a region where there is high unemployment. You know that these workers are unlikely to find employment elsewhere if the plant closes down. You are also convinced that the plant is safe: you work there, and you know it is checked regularly and that equipment is monitored and updated when necessary.

You are worried that if the plant is closed down, there will not be any investment to reskill and reintegrate the workers. They will be in the same position as thousands of other unemployed people in the region.

Members of the Stop Nuclear Energy group

Your group is against nuclear energy and has protested against the plant ever since it was built. You think that nuclear energy is unnecessary, expensive and dangerous – both for the planet and for people. We have all heard about Fukushima, but there have been more than 20 nuclear accidents or incidents. You are worried that this nuclear plant is relatively old and that it now poses serious risks for local inhabitants. Furthermore, many people are unaware that uranium is no longer being mined in your country: it comes from countries where people are being exploited and their lands are taken away to be used for mining. Uranium mining leaves dead lands behind.

Further, the risk of destroying the aquifer below NeoClear is huge, and your region is in danger of losing its main drinking water supply.

You want to send a message to the representatives of the workers at NeoClear: closing the nuclear plant can allow new jobs to be created in more sustainable energy fields. This will mean more work and greater safety for you and your children!

Members of EF – Energy for the Future

You represent the company managing the nuclear plant at the moment. You have invested time and money in this plant, and it has supplied homes and industry in the region with energy, and offered employment to 2 000 local people. Your company carries out regular safety checks and risk assessments and you know that everything is in order. The plant poses no threat to the environment or to people's health.

If the worst comes about and the decision is made to close the plant, you want to be sure that all shareholders in the company are fully compensated for any losses. The company should not have to pay for decommissioning the plant and should not have to pay compensation to workers.

Members of the Windland Parliament

Your parliament decided recently that all nuclear plants on the territory of Windland had to be closed within 10 years. You were invited to Floville to give testimony explaining why you voted to close down nuclear plants in your country.

Your main reasons for voting to close down nuclear plants were that uranium is not sustainable and will be depleted in the not-too-distant future. All this technology will then become useless. You decided that it is much more worthwhile to invest in sustainable energies like wind or the sun, than to continue subsidising the nuclear sector.

You want to give a strong political signal related to the risks that NeoClear poses to people in Windland, as the border is just 2 km from the plant. You think closing down NeoClear is an important step towards clean energy throughout the region.

Role card: Citizens of Floville

You are worried about the conflict related to the closing down of the plant. There are good arguments for and against on each side. At the moment you do not know what you will vote for: you need to speak to as many different groups as you can and then you plan to make up your mind.

OUR FUTURES

This activity is an adaptation of "Our futures" from "Compass: manual for human rights education with young people", Council of Europe (2012).

Overview

This is a creative activity, where participants design and draw a model for an ideal development in their community.

Key concepts

Health, planning, local environment, development, community

Complexity: Level 2

Group size: 6+

Time: 60 minutes

Objectives

▶ to understand some of the considerations involved in urban (re)development;

▶ to develop creativity, group work skills, co-operation and respect for others;

▶ to develop skills necessary for participating in local democracy and development.

Materials

▶ paper for drafts;

▶ large sheets of paper for the final design;

▶ paints, brushes, pencils, pens and markers;

▶ materials for a collage, e.g. coloured paper, magazines, twigs, rice, beans, dead leaves, shells, drinking straws;

▶ scissors;

▶ glue and tape;

▶ pictures or photographs of how the neighbourhood/town looked 10 or 20 years ago (optional);

▶ maps of where you live, both old and new maps (optional).

Preparation

▶ make sure that you have plenty of materials for making the models. Start saving small containers, inner tubes from toilet rolls, etc. well in advance of starting this activity;

▶ you could prepare participants by encouraging them to walk around their locality, noting things they would have done differently, if they had been responsible for development.

Instructions

1. Introduce the concept of change over time. Ask participants to think back to when they were younger and what their homes and local streets looked like, and how they have changed.

    –   Have any of the rooms in the school or centre where you meet been redecorated, or is there any new furniture?

    –   Are there new buildings in the neighbourhood, e.g. shopping centres, housing estates, roads, play parks or cycle tracks?

    –   Has the road layout changed, is there more or less traffic, are there any special arrangements for pedestrians or cyclists?

2. Ask people why these things have changed and who made the decisions about what should be renewed and how it should be done. For example, did a particular housing scheme provide much-needed, low-cost housing for local people or was it luxury apartments or holiday homes built as an investment by a finance company?

3. Briefly discuss 1 or 2 examples, using some of the following questions:
    - who benefited from the way this was developed?
    - who decided, and how? If any of the changes are seen as negative by participants, ask them what they would have done had they been in control.

4. Ask people to get into groups of 3-4. Give each group some paper and pens, and ask it to draft or sketch ideas for its ideal neighbourhood/town of the future. Participants are only limited by their imaginations.

5. When each group has agreed on a draft plan, it should transfer it onto a large sheet of paper and complete it with paint and collage materials.

6. When the work is done, ask each group in turn to present its plan and say where it got its ideas from and how it developed them. Allow time for short questions and answers after each presentation, but leave general discussion for the debriefing.

Debriefing

Start with a review of how the different groups worked.

▶ Did everyone feel involved? How were decisions made?

Then go on to talk about the plans themselves.

▶ What were the main considerations when deciding how to develop the site, e.g. cost, time, effort, profit, local needs, aesthetics?

▶ Were the plans people-friendly? Were they sustainable?

▶ Did the plans meet the needs of everyone in the locality, e.g. the disabled, children, minorities, the poor and marginalised?

▶ Was your plan very demanding in terms of material resources, e.g. lots of building materials?

▶ Were renewable resources used whenever possible?

▶ How would the project affect the ecosystem in general? For example, did you think about wildlife? Were trees planted?

▶ How much waste would be produced building the project and in maintaining it? How would this waste be disposed of?

Tips for facilitators

The title of this activity is "Our futures". In using the plural, the intention is to emphasise that the future is not predetermined, rather that it is what we make it. There are many possible futures and the challenge for young people is to build a future which reflects their ideals and aspirations.

To reinforce the concept of change, you may like to show old pictures of how the local area looked 10 or 20 years ago. You can also ask them to think of global changes. For instance, they should think about the fact that 50 years ago, the internet was the stuff of science fiction.

If participants are not sure about what their future town may be like, you could prompt them by asking the following questions.

▶ Who will live here? People born here or newcomers? How old will they be? Will they live in families?

▶ What will their daily lives be like? Where will they shop for food? How will they travel around?

▶ What sort of welfare services, such as medical and housing services, will they need?

▶ What will their schools be like?

▶ How will they travel?

▶ What will the houses be like?

▶ What will their social lives be like? What will they do in their leisure time?

▶ Will they have pets?

- How, or where, will people work?
- What new technological developments might there be?
- What about the environment? The natural surroundings?

As an alternative, you could allow participants to choose a real site in their locality which they would like to develop, or develop differently. For example, what would they rather see on the site where the town hall, council offices, hospital, etc. now stand? Or if you live in a rural locality, what better use could there be for a disued pit or a slag heap left over from mining operations? Use the story "Garden in a night" to motivate them!

Suggestions for follow-up

You could explore how your locality could adapt itself to the future challenge of climate change. The Transition Town initiative involves local people looking at all aspects of their community (food, energy, transport, health, heart and soul, economics and livelihoods, etc.) and finding creative ways to launch a community-defined, community-implemented Energy Descent Action Plan over a 15 to 20-year timescale. Initiatives so far have included creating community gardens to grow food, a business waste exchange (which seeks to match the waste of one industry with another industry that uses this waste), repairing old items rather than throwing them away, and developing local exchange trading systems. For more information and examples of how people are developing this concept all over the world, see https://transitionnetwork.org/ or put "Transition Towns" into your search engine.

As a follow-up activity, you could try the activity "NeoClear Inc.", which simulates a community debate on forms of energy.

Ideas for action

Make an exhibition of the collages and invite local councillors to come and hear your views.

Get a copy of the strategy plans (annual and long term) for your community. Analyse them within the group and then consult with friends and family. Give your feedback by creating a blog, writing to a local newspaper, organising a public meeting on this issue or participating in a public assembly organised by the authorities.

Background information – Garden in a night

At the Copenhagen City of Culture Festival in 1996, a group of young people presented the project "Have på en nat" ("Garden in a night"). They were from Økologiske Igangsættere, a local Agenda 21 organisation, and had worked for two years preparing to build a garden on a derelict inner city site – not quite in one night – but over a few days. The young people decided that they wanted a community garden on the 300-square metre site. They learned practical skills such as carpentry, plumbing, bricklaying and horticulture and prepared and grew everything off-site, so that when the time came the garden could be assembled almost "overnight". There was something for everyone: little paths wound around the site by a turfed area, trees, shrubs, flowers and vegetables. The garden remained until the site was reclaimed by the council to be developed for housing in April 2001.

STOP CLIMATE CHAOS

This activity is an adaptation from the resource pack "The Sustainable Development Goals and youth", National Youth Council of Ireland (2015).

Overview

This is a lively introductory activity in which participants learn about climate change through a competitive teamwork game.

Key concepts

Climate change, weather, global warming effects, Europe

Complexity: Level 1

Group size: 12+

Time: 45 minutes

Objectives

- ► to learn about some of the causes and effects of climate change;
- ► to discuss young people's relation to these causes and effects;
- ► to help with group building.

Materials

- ► balloons;
- ► paper, art materials, markers.

Preparation

Put a statement from page 84 into each of the balloons, and blow them up. Each participant needs 1 balloon.

Instructions

1. Divide participants into two teams and ask them to line up, one person behind the other. Place a chair between each team and the balloons in 2 piles at the head of the lines.

2. On your signal, the teams pass the balloons backwards over their heads to the end of the line. The last person has to sit on the balloon until it bursts. S/he collects the statement and runs to the front of the line. Keep playing until all the balloons are burst.

3. Bring everyone back together and in the large group, ask each person to read out their statement. Some of the statements will be repeated, but it will still be useful to read them out.

4. Bring the group back together for the debriefing.

Debriefing

Begin by asking if people were surprised by any of the statements. Was there anything "new" in the statements?
- ► Which pieces of information were most shocking?
- ► Who is contributing most to climate change? Who is least responsible?
- ► Where are the effects mostly being felt?
- ► As the next generation, do you think it is fair that this is the world you are inheriting?
- ► Could something still be done about it? Who does it depend on?
- ► What could you do – either as individuals, or as a group?

Suggestions for follow-up

The activity "Climate superhero auditions" looks at the different groups and actors in society whose support is needed if we are to make a difference in tackling climate change.

The activity "Our futures" is a creative activity in which participants build a model of their ideal future city.

Ideas for action

Support participants to find out what their government is doing to address climate change. If their country is part of the EU – are they meeting the 2020 targets? If not part of the EU, would the country be on track to meet such targets?

The same research could be carried out at local level: participants could contact local representatives to find out what is being done, for example, by the local council, to switch to renewable energy, reduce consumption and cut down on greenhouse gas emissions. They could then form a petition, or try to raise awareness among other young people locally so that their voice is better heard.

Handout: climate change cards

Climate change affects every aspect of society, from the health of the global economy to the health of our children. It is about the water in our wells and in our taps. It is about the food on the table. It is at the core of nearly all the major challenges we face today (UN Secretary-General Ban Ki-moon, Opening remarks to the World Business Summit on Climate Change, 24 May 2009).

Climate change is leading to an increase in extreme weather events such as hurricanes, floods and tornados, while the rains are failing in many countries, leading to drought.

Agriculture is one of the sectors expected to be affected most by climate change. Water shortages and extreme weather events make planting and harvesting of crops very difficult and can lead to a reduction in both the yield and quality of produce.

The cause of climate change is man-made, with increased emissions of greenhouse gases due to burning of fossil fuels (coal, oil and gas) and also deforestation of tropical rainforests. Agriculture also contributes through methane (cows belching) and nitrous oxide emissions (mainly through nitrogen losses from fertilisers and manure).

We now know with 97% certainty that burning fossil fuels is causing global warming and climate change. That is the same level of certainty we have that smoking causes cancer.

Oceans have warmed, the amounts of snow and ice have diminished and sea levels have risen. From 1901 to 2010, the global average sea level rose by 19 cm as oceans expanded due to warming and ice melted.

The price of solar photovoltaic panels is plummeting, making it a viable technology even in countries of the North. A solar panel in Dublin yields 80% of the electricity of a solar panel in Madrid, thanks to longer daylight hours. During a recent heatwave in the UK, solar provided 15% of the country's electricity.

Changing weather patterns and extreme weather events are already a reality for communities in many developing countries. It is estimated that by 2025, almost two thirds of the world's population (5.4 billion people) are likely to experience some kind of water stress, and for 1 billion of them the water shortage will be severe.

Although the EU as a whole is still on track to meet its 2020 climate and energy targets, by 2015 only 16 member states were in a position to deliver on all three national targets (greenhouse gas emissions, use of renewables and energy consumption).

The European region, consisting of 52 countries, bears a significant responsibility for its historical contributions to global warming. This region is home to six of today's top 20 annual global CO_2 emitters.

Extreme weather events are becoming more frequent and more severe, threatening the reliability and productivity of agriculture, making worse already extreme levels of poverty, and reinforcing chronic undernutrition.

The world's poorest countries have done the least to cause climate change but they are being hit first and hardest by its impacts and are least able to adapt.

SUSTAINABILITY BINGO

Overview

This is a fast-moving activity for participants to get to know each other, and reflect on their own relationship to sustainability.

Key concepts

Sustainability, lifestyle, recycling

Complexity: Level 1

Group size: 12+

Time: 15-30 minutes

Objectives

- ▶ for participants to get to know each other;
- ▶ to examine personal attitudes towards sustainability;
- ▶ to assess lifestyle actions and choices in relation to sustainability.

Materials

- ▶ copies of the bingo sheet for each participant;
- ▶ pens.

Instructions

1. Show participants the bingo sheet, and explain that the aim of the activity is to answer each question on the sheet with the names of other participants. Give them an example:

   > If Freda keeps and reuses plastic bags, I write Freda's name next to this question. Then I look for someone else to answer another question.

2. Emphasise that they can only write each person's name once on the sheet: they need 12 different people to win the game. When they have 12 answers, from 12 different people, they should shout "Bingo" – and the game stops.

3. Give everyone a copy of the bingo sheet and a pen. Tell them to stand up, and start collecting answers from others in the group.

4. When the first person shouts bingo, stop the game and invite everyone back while the answers are checked. Go through the winning sheet quickly, making sure there are no duplicate names – and that the answers are satisfactory.

5. Announce the winner, or if there are significant problems with the first sheet completed, ask if anyone filled out 11 boxes, then if necessary 10 boxes – and go through one of those sheets.

6. If time allows, discuss some of the questions in more detail, or use some of the following debriefing questions.

Debriefing and evaluation

- ▶ What have you learned about other people in this group?
- ▶ Have you learned anything about yourself? What were these questions about?
- ▶ Do you think any of them were not relevant to the idea of sustainability? Which, and why?
- ▶ What does sustainability mean to you?
- ▶ Which of the questions do you think were most important? Why?

Tips for facilitators

You can use this as a quick introductory activity with a new group, so that participants get to know each other. Or you can use it with an existing group to introduce the idea of sustainability. If time allows, you can introduce some of the information on sustainability from Chapter 2.

If you find that the first person to finish has filled out some answers incorrectly, or used the same name more than once, you could turn to others in the group who came close to filling out their grids. Do not worry too much if there is no absolute winner – the main purpose is for participants to start a discussion with each other on the theme of sustainability.

If no one has finished after about 10 minutes, call for a break, and see which participant has filled out the most questions.

Use some of the background information in Chapter 2 to support participants' understanding of sustainability.

Suggestions for follow-up

The activity "Chicken sandwich" looks in more detail at sustainability, particularly in relation to food and agriculture.

"Fishing game" is a simulation of the way commercial fishing works, and gives participants the opportunity to look at the sustainability of fishing in our oceans.

Ideas for action

Ask participants to try to do one thing before the next meeting to lessen their own – or others' – impact on the planet. This could be taken from the bingo sheet, or could be on the initiative of participants.

You could also look at the list of actions from Chapter 5 and select together with participants an action for the group to work on together.

Handout: sustainability bingo

Find someone who...

Is vegan or vegetarian Name:	Looks at where food has come from before buying it Name:	Has taken a train or coach instead of flying in the last 12 months (find out why) Name:
Has eaten something they have grown themselves Name:	Can name an organisation working on environmental issues Name:	Keeps and reuses plastic bags Name:
Owns something which has been recycled Name:	Has taken part in a campaign or activity relating to climate change Name:	Has tweeted or posted an article relating to the environment Name:
Has made a change in his/her life for environmental reasons Name:	Has spent time in a forest or with nature in the last 2 weeks Name:	Can recommend a film or song about the environment Name:

TAKE A STEP FORWARD

This activity is adapted from "Compass: manual for human rights education with young people", Council of Europe (2012).

Overview

In this activity participants take on roles and move forward depending on their chances and opportunities in life.

Key concepts

Climate change, environmental degradation, pollution, inequality

Complexity: Level 2

Group size: 10-30

Time: 60 minutes

Objectives

- ▶ to raise awareness about the effects of environmental degradation on people's living conditions and particularly of climate change;
- ▶ to raise awareness about the connection between unsustainable practices in the developed countries and social and environmental injustice worldwide;
- ▶ to foster empathy and solidarity with vulnerable people.

Materials

- ▶ role cards;
- ▶ a large open space (a corridor, large room or outdoors);
- ▶ a hat or a bowl.

Preparation

Read the instructions carefully. Review the list of "situations and events" and adapt them, if necessary, for the group that you are working with.

Prepare the role cards, 1 per participant. Copy the cards, cut out the strips, fold them in half and put them in a hat. Keep back any you want to give to particular participants (see Tips for facilitators).

Instructions

1. Create a calm atmosphere with some soft background music, or ask the participants for silence.
2. Ask participants to take a role card out of the hat. Tell them to keep it to themselves and not show it to anyone else.
3. Invite them to sit down (preferably on the floor) and read their card (again) carefully.
4. Now ask them to begin to get into character. To help, read out some of the following questions, pausing after each, to give people time to reflect and build up a picture of themselves and their lives.
    - What is your everyday life like now?
    - Where do you socialise?
    - What do you do in the morning, in the afternoon, in the evening?
    - What sort of lifestyle do you have?
    - Where do you live?
    - What do you do in your leisure time?
    - What you do during your holidays?
    - How much time do you spend in nature or outdoors?
5. Now ask people to remain absolutely silent as they line up beside each other (as if at a starting line).

6. Tell them that you are going to read out a list of situations or events. If they think that their character can answer "yes" to a statement, they should take a step forward. Otherwise, they should stay where they are and not move.

7. Read out the situations one at a time. Pause for a while between each statement to allow people time to step forward. Remind them to look around (silently) at where others are standing.

8. When you have read out all the statements, invite participants to take note of their final positions in comparison to the rest of the group. Call them back to the circle and bring them out of character before debriefing the activity in plenary. You can bring them out of character, for example, by telling them to shout out their real names on the count of 3.

Debriefing

Start by asking participants for their general reactions to the activity. Then use some of the following questions to explore issues in more detail. Select those which are most relevant to your group – do not attempt to address all of them.

- ▶ How did people feel when they took a step forward – or when they didn't?
- ▶ For those who stepped forward often, at what point did they begin to notice that others were not moving as fast as they were?
- ▶ Did anyone feel that the situation was not fair?
- ▶ Can anyone guess anything about someone else's role?

Let people reveal their roles during this part of the discussion, and tell participants that all roles were based on real examples.

- ▶ How easy or difficult was it to play your role? What made it difficult?
- ▶ If you were in your own (real) character, would you have stepped forward differently?
- ▶ Are you surprised by the difficulties that environmental issues are having on people's everyday lives? Were you aware of this before the activity?
- ▶ Does the exercise mirror life in any way? Why, or why not?
- ▶ Can you think of any steps that could be taken to address some of these issues?

Tips for facilitators

Select the cards and statements which will be most relevant for your group. You can also create some of your own to reflect their local reality.

You could make a globe or maps of the world available to participants so that they can see roughly where "they" are from.

Be sensitive to any roles which might be difficult for certain participants for personal reasons, or otherwise.

In the first stage, when participants are imagining themselves into their roles, it is possible that some may say that they know little about the life of the person they have to play. Tell them that they can use their imagination to fill out the picture – and that it does not matter if there are inaccuracies.

Suggestions for follow-up

The activity "Chain reactions" looks at how small actions people take – particularly in richer countries – can have a fatal effect on people in other parts of the globe. Participants could even try to draw their own chain from actions in their community to the actions described on some of the cards.

Ideas for action

Show participants the map from the background information "Climate change in Europe". Discuss the probable consequences of climate change on their region. Some consequences may be positive – for example, a longer growing season in northern regions. Others will be negative, but this may not immediately be obvious to participants – for example, the northern movement of species. You could draw a problem tree with the group, identifying both the causes and effects of climate change. Use this to identify local issues that the group could campaign on.

Encourage participants to research further the case study on their own card, or to select a few cases as a group and look into the issues described. Then support them to find out whether there are organisations campaigning on these issues – for example, on lead pollution in Zambia or waste from gold mining in Romania. You could even make contact with such campaigning organisations, or invite someone from a local organisation to speak to the group.

Background information – Climate change in Europe

Figure 12. Climate change in Europe

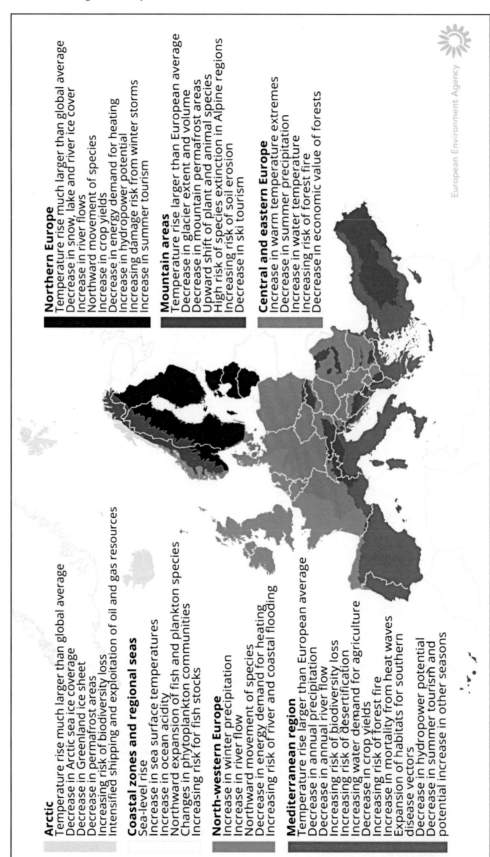

Source: European Environment Agency (2017)

Handout: role cards

You are 17 and you live in a small village in Romania. The village is 5 km away from a goldmine, which produces huge amounts of toxic waste because of the chemicals used in mining. Vegetation around your village has slowly died, and the surrounding hills are no longer covered by forests. The water has a strange taste.

You are 17 and you live in a small village in Austria in beautiful natural surroundings. People in the area are mostly well-off, and place high importance on having a strong community and healthy lifestyle. Local farms mostly use organic farming practices.

You are 16 and you live in South Africa. Your parents work in a mine not far from your house, under very difficult conditions. Your father often complains of chest pains and coughs, and your mother has a nasty skin complaint. The water has a strange taste.

You are 15 and you live in a ghetto at the margins of a small city in Italy, close to a massive rubbish tip and next to the motorway. Most of the ghetto residents are unemployed; many work by rummaging through the rubbish tip.

You are 15 and you live in a big city in Linfen, China, where there is a serious problem with pollution. The town is often enveloped in thick, filthy smog, and that makes breathing very difficult. It often triggers an asthma attack for you. When there's a smog alert, you normally do not go to school.

You are 24 and you are a farmer in Morocco. It is becoming increasingly difficult to make a living as a farmer: there have been severe droughts and the summer temperatures have broken records since you took over your father's smallholding. Last year was not the first year that you lost most of your crops as a result of the weather.

You are 16 and you live in a tower block on the outskirts of a city in Britain. Your neighbourhood is grey, noisy and has little in the way of entertainment. There are no parks or squares and the motorway is just next to the block where you live.

You are 16 and you live in Puerto Rico. Your family lost everything in a recent hurricane. Your house and everything inside was destroyed. Most of the town was under water for several days, and there is still no electricity, no phone network and no water supply. Many of your friends have disappeared; they are probably among the dead.

You are 14 and you live in a village close to a nuclear plant. Only once has the alarm been raised at the plant, and the authorities said that everything was put right straight away. There are often campaigners outside the plant saying that it is old and dangerous and needs to be closed down.

You are 13 and you live in the Czech Republic, close to a river which has been heavily polluted by an industrial site nearby. Children often swim in the river in summer. You have often seen dead fish in it.

You are 14 and you live by the Citarum River in Indonesia. You have been told that this is the most polluted river in the world, but it still provides drinking water for 5 million people. You sometimes notice that the water has a strange colour.

You are 15 and you live in India, close to a leather tannery which leaves a terrible stench in the air, day and night. Your dad used to work in the factory, but he died last year from cancer. Lots of the workers die from cancer. The nearby river is also polluted by the tannery.

You are 16 and you live in Mailuu-Suu, in Kyrgyzstan, not far from an area where radioactive waste has been stored for many years. Life expectancy is 10 years less than the national average in this area.

You are 50 and you live in La Oroya, Peru, next to a metal processing plant. The air is polluted by lead emissions from the factory, and lung problems are very common among local residents. Children also suffer from respiratory complications.

You are 20 and you live not far from Kabwe, in Zambia. The main industry is lead mining, but although this provides employment, it means that local people have about 10 times more lead in their bodies than they should. Because of the mining, nothing grows on the hills anymore.

You are 65 and you live in a small village next to the Amazonian forest in Brazil. Recently, intensive deforestation for industrial purposes has destroyed much of the forest. Landscapes are not the same as they were when you were young. All day long, heavy trucks pass by where you live.

You are 20 and you live in a heavily polluted city of about 20 million inhabitants. This year, for about 3 weeks, the air was heavy and full of pollution from traffic and industrial activities. A thick layer of smog covered the city.

You are 16 and you live in the Congo, on the outskirts of a big city. The water is often contaminated and sanitation is still a problem.

You are 15 and you live in a small village on the coast of Japan. You want to become a fisherman. Unfortunately, most of the fish is contaminated. People say it is because of the Fukushima nuclear accident some years ago.

You are 15 and you live on the island of Kiribati. Many of the islanders are afraid that because of sea level rise, your island will disappear in the next 100 years, or even sooner.

You are 18 and you live in Samoa, an island of less than 3 000 square kilometres. Because of ocean warming, coral reefs are dying, and risk disappearing altogether from the coasts around your island. These reefs protect your island from the sea, which otherwise would erode the coastline. People say that sea level rise is going to lead to your island disappearing in the next 100 years.

You are 15 and you live in Paris, France. Every spring you suffer from hay fever. Your apartment is not far from one of the main roads into Paris, which gets very busy and very noisy during the day.

You are 50 and you live in a village next to a lake in Alaska, USA. There have been extraordinary changes in the climate and the natural environment over your lifetime. Many of the birds you saw in your childhood have now disappeared, and recently there have been terrible droughts and an increase in wildfires.

You are 48 and you live in a village near Tomsk, in Siberian Russia. Winters used to be really cold when you were young, but recently they have become less extreme and the growing season seems longer.

You are 33 and you live in the Coimbra district of Portugal. You have seen terrible droughts and wildfires in recent years, and your friends are worried things will get worse with global warming. But you are not worried because you have a lovely second home in a picturesque town in Norway.

List of statements

Read out the following statements. Allow time after each one so that participants can step forward and look around at the rest of the group.

- ▸ You have access to healthy food.
- ▸ The air you breathe is healthy.
- ▸ The water you drink is clean and pure.
- ▸ You have never suffered from allergies or asthma.
- ▸ You can relax in a nice natural environment not far from where you live.
- ▸ You have heard about droughts, but you have never really experienced one. Water has always been in good supply.
- ▸ You could easily grow your own vegetables at or near your home.
- ▸ The weather is temperate: there are no extreme weather events.
- ▸ You are not worried about your health.
- ▸ The flora and fauna next to where you live are healthy, and mostly unchanged over the past few decades.
- ▸ You know that the place where you live has a clean and safe environment.
- ▸ In your daily life you do not think about changes to the natural environment.
- ▸ You do not worry about climate change.
- ▸ There is nothing in your immediate environment which will make it difficult for you to earn a living.
- ▸ You are positive about your future and you think you will live long!

THE COST OF FASHION

This activity is an adaptation of "Beware we are watching" from "Compass: manual for human rights education with young people" (Council of Europe 2012).

Overview

In this activity participants learn about the social, economic and environmental costs of a cotton T-shirt. They then go on to plan and implement action to address the related environmental issues.

Key concepts

Sustainability, consumerism, clothing, waste, pollution, carbon emissions

Complexity: Level 3

Group size: 6+

Time: Part 1: 45 minutes (this part can be run by itself); Parts 2 and 3: 1-3 hours

Objectives

- ▶ to learn about the globalised nature of the clothing industry and appreciate the environmental cost of the clothes we buy;
- ▶ to develop skills to analyse information, plan and implement action;
- ▶ to encourage creativity, imagination and a commitment to activism.

Materials

- ▶ flip chart and marker pens;
- ▶ the information on pages 97-98.

Preparation

Make copies of the information on page 98. You will need 1 copy per participant.

Instructions

Part 1: Looking at the issues

1. Explain that the group is going to take a closer look at the clothes its members buy, and the social, economic and environmental impacts of their choices.

2. Ask participants to look at the labels on their T-shirts or sweaters to see where they were made and what they are made from. What did they cost? Make a table on the flip chart, listing the materials, countries and prices.

3. Ask if money is the only cost to be considered when buying a T-shirt. Then hand out the information sheet on page 98 and give participants 15 minutes to read and discuss it in small groups.

4. Bring the groups back together and ask for participants' reactions to the information. Use some of the questions below to debrief the information and prepare for the next stage.

Debriefing (Part 1)

- ▶ Will this information make a difference to you when you buy T-shirts in the future? Why, or why not?
- ▶ Which other "costs" can you list when buying a T-shirt (apart from price)?
- ▶ Which considerations (or costs) do you think are most important when buying a T-shirt? Why?
- ▶ How can you persuade other people that these considerations are important?
- ▶ How can you persuade them to do something about it?

Part 2: Planning for action

You could refer to the chapter "Making a difference" to support this activity.

5.   Ask participants what they could do – both as individuals, and as a group – to address some of the issues discussed. Give them ideas to start them off, if necessary: e.g. take better care of their clothes so that they do not wear out so quickly, buy only fair-trade T-shirts in the future, buy second-hand clothes, launch a campaign in their locality to raise awareness about the issues among their peers, launch a campaign on social media. Make a list of all the suggestions.

6.   Discuss which ideas they would most like to take forward. You could select several, allow them to research for more information and think about the feasibility of the selected ideas.

7.   Make a final choice as a group, or choose 2-3 actions to be carried out in small groups. Then draw up a plan for each proposed action. This should include:

      –   a clear aim: the end goal;

      –   a series of achievable objectives, as steps on the way to the goal;

      –   a description of the proposed activity (boycott, concerts, television or radio programmes, street theatre, leafleting, etc.), including reasons for their choice;

      –   the places where the activity will take place (schools, public buildings, etc.);

      –   a timetable for preparing the activity and implementing it;

      –   estimated costs and resources needed.

8.   Ask each group to submit its proposals and ask everyone to comment and make suggestions for improvements.

Debriefing (Part 2)

▶ How easy was it to agree on an action plan within your group?

▶ Is everyone happy with the plan, and happy about the way the decisions were made in the small groups? Why? Why not?

▶ Why did people choose the action they did?

▶ Does everyone feel involved? Why? Why not?

▶ Which issues are the different groups targeting?

Part 3: Implementation

▶ either choose one action for the whole group to participate in, or let participants work in small groups according to the action they want to take;

▶ at the end of the action or campaign, review how it went and what the group achieved.

Debriefing (Part 3)

▶ How did the action or campaign go? Did it go according to plan? Why? Why not?

▶ What do you think you achieved?

▶ What do you need to remember for next time?

▶ Did everyone feel involved and their abilities used? If not, why and what could be done better next time?

▶ What else have you learned from doing the activity and from taking action?

Suggestions for follow-up

The group may be interested to explore the issues and dilemmas relating to corporate social responsibility. For example, many good causes and events receive sponsorship from companies that are responsible for human rights violations. These companies may also be polluting the environment in the process of manufacturing goods. The group could discuss the issues raised in the following statement by Jeremy Gilley, filmmaker and founder of Peace One Day:

> From Peace One Day's point of view, we could not exist or function without corporate sponsorship. My position is very clear. I feel strongly that in order to influence the supply chain we have to be "in the room". It's very difficult, perhaps impossible to find a company whose entire supply chain from top to bottom complies 100% with international human rights/trade law, although of course this is a position which is desirable.

More information about this initiative can be found at www.peaceoneday.org.

The activity "Greenwashing" looks at the way companies mask the damage they are doing to the environment with an environmentally friendly message.

Ideas for action

One action rarely meets all its objectives! You could discuss ways to follow up on the action already carried out by the group, so as to keep up the pressure. This might involve carrying out one of the other plans developed in the small group work, or could involve the whole group thinking about how it could build on the first initiative.

Background information – The environmental cost of clothing

- the "carbon footprint" of a single T-shirt is estimated to be around 6 kg, i.e. around 20 times its own weight! Source: https://www.domain-b.com/environment/20090403_carbon_footprint.html;

- according to the Carbon Trust, clothing in general accounts for around 3% of the global production (or 850 million metric tonnes) of CO_2 emissions per year. This figure includes both the production process and emissions produced after we have bought the clothing, such as when we are washing, drying and ironing. Source: http://goodonyou.eco;

- the estimated annual global textile production is 60 billion kg of fabric. Based on this, the total energy and water needed to produce the total global production of fabric is estimated to be 1 074 billion KWh of electricity (or 132 million metric tonnes of coal) and 6-9 trillion litres of water. Source: http://bit.ly/2wfEs7A;

- an estimated 17-20% of industrial water pollution comes from textile dyeing and treatment and an estimated 8 000 synthetic chemicals are used throughout the world to turn raw materials into textiles, many of which will be released into freshwater sources. Source: http://bit.ly/2mlnFMu.

Handout: tracking the true cost of cotton

Cotton T-shirts are the product of a number of different global industries, with production in almost every country in the world. Here is how it might work:

A typical cotton farm in Burkina Faso is a freehold, worked on by a family which cultivates the 6-8 hectares of land. A kilo of Burkina Faso-produced raw cotton is worth €0.23. For many of the cotton producers the money they get from selling the cotton is the only cash they receive in the whole year.

From the farm, the cotton is transported to the ginning factory to make lint, a process which takes the cost per kilo to €0.56. Workers are paid €73.40 every fortnight.

The cotton is now transported for export to the Togo port of Lome, where it is sold to merchants at €0.88 per kilo. Over half of it is sold to China: it is loaded onto cargo ships for ports such as Shanghai, where it is sold to local spinning factories for €0.97 per kilo. Most of the workers on the line come from poorer areas, often in China's vast rural hinterland. They live in dormitories in the factory and work very long hours for low pay.

The garments themselves – made for many of the West's most famous brands, often in the same massive factory as where the yarn is spun – are now taken to a port and loaded for export. The average price of a T-shirt imported into the US is €1.10, but a downtown department store in Manhattan will sell two for €14.70.

Cotton that started in Africa costing €0.56 a kilo is now worth €18.40 a kilo.

Source: *Tracking the true cost of cotton*, BBC News (2007), available at http://bbc.in/2Frxotu.

The true cost of one cotton T-shirt

Taking a range of environmental costs into consideration:

► water: it can take more than 20 000 litres of water to produce 1 kg of cotton, which is roughly the weight of a single T-shirt and pair of jeans. Water use is at least 2 157 litres (45% is used for irrigation);

► energy use: 8 kilowatt hours of electricity for spinning and sewing machines. This is equivalent to the energy used by a domestic clothes washing machine running for 16 hours;

► greenhouse gas emissions: 10.75 kg of CO_2 and other greenhouse gases. This is 50 times heavier than the shirt itself, and equivalent to a 40-km drive by car;

► other gas emissions:
  – nitric oxide and nitrogen dioxide contribute to smog and acid rain;
  – sulphur dioxide, a major air pollutant, can lead to respiratory illness;
  – carbon monoxide is toxic in high concentrations;

► fuel: 41.6-110 litres for transport by land and sea. This is the same as a 32-km car journey (for the upper limit);

► transport distances: 5 000-12 000 km, depending on where the cotton is grown and the shirt is made. From the Hebei Province in China to the centre of Prague is 7 500 km;

► toxins: 1-3 g pesticides, diesel exhaust, heavy metals (dyes);

► cost on import: €0.44-0.77;

► child labour: in 17 countries, the average wage is €0.37 per day;

► miscellaneous: 53-91 g of fertiliser.

Sources: http://true-cost.re-configure.org/ and Worldwide Fund for Nature, wwf.panda.org/about_our_earth/about_freshwater/freshwater_problems/thirsty_crops/cotton/

THUMBS UP, THUMBS DOWN

Overview

An energiser with discussion to explore the idea of competition and the relation to sustainability.

Key concepts

Competition, collaboration, consumerism

Complexity: Level 1

Group size: Any

Time: 15-30 minutes

Objectives

▶ to prompt discussion on issues relating to competition, collaboration and consumerism.

Preparation

Make sure participants can sit in pairs.

Instructions

1. Ask participants to link hands with the person sitting next to them. Hands should be clasped so the fingers of each hand curl over each other. The thumbs should remain upright (see Figure 13).

2. Explain that you can only move your thumb (on the clasped hand), and the objective of the game is to get your partner's thumb lying flat across your index finger. You score a point each time you manage to do this.

Figure 13. The exercise in practice

3. Give the signal to begin and allow pairs at least 5 minutes to see what strategies are used.

4. Announce the end of the game, and ask people to raise their hands if they scored:
   - more than 3?
   - more than 5?
   - more than 10?

Source: Wikimedia, https://commons.wikimedia.org/wiki/File:Thumb_Wrestling.jpg

Debriefing

Use some of the following questions to discuss the activity.

Reflections on the activity.

▶ Who won? How do you know?

▶ Was it meant to be a competition? How do you know? Who were you competing against?

▶ What strategy did you use?

At this point, if any of the pairs used a strategy of collaboration – for example, agreeing that partners allow each other to score, thus increasing the total score – ask these pairs to talk about their strategy. If no pairs did this, ask what would have happened if there had been collaboration.

▶ Would the score have been higher?

▶ Do you think you would have felt any differently towards your partner?

Reflections on the wider meaning.

> ▸ Why did (most of) you assume that you were competing?
>
> ▸ Do you think competition or collaboration is more "natural"? Why? Do you collaborate or compete with your friends more often?
>
> ▸ Can you give examples of collaboration in real life – examples where competition would make life impossible?

You could offer examples such as: parents competing with their children, a youth worker (or teacher) competing with the young people, or workers making different components for a car or computer in competition with each other.

> ▸ Can you think of examples of competition in real life? What is good about it? What is bad about it?
>
> ▸ How is competition related to sustainability?

Prompt them by suggesting that competition and consumerism are linked. You could give the example of mobile phone companies putting out new models constantly, in order to beat their competitors.

> ▸ Can you think of ways in which more collaboration would help to address issues of sustainability?

Tips for facilitators

When giving the initial instructions, try to avoid calling it a thumb wrestle or competition.

If one pair is familiar with the activity, or guesses quickly that collaboration leads to higher scores, you could call an end to the game after just a few minutes. If no one works it out, do not go on too long: the discussion is the most important part of the activity.

Suggestions for follow-up

The activity "Waste manifesto" looks at the problem of waste and pollution, often directly related to increasing consumerism. Alternatively, you could use the activity "Greenwashing" to explore the messages that companies put out in order that people buy their products (and in order that the damage to the environment is hidden).

The activity "Fishing game" is a simulation game, involving competing fishers. The activity illustrates how depletion of the seas can come about if competition and profit are the only considerations.

Ideas for action

Let participants select one of the actions from Chapter 5 – or another of their own choosing – to be undertaken by the whole group. Use this to illustrate the importance of everyone working together towards a common goal. When the action has been completed, get participants to reflect on the balance between competition and collaboration in the planning and implementation of the activity.

WASTE MANIFESTO

Overview

The activity involves discussion in groups followed by a practical planning activity to produce a strategy on waste for the group.

Key concepts

Consumerism, waste, pollution, ecological footprint, recycling

Complexity: Level 2

Group size: 6-30

Time: Part 1: 40 minutes; Part 2: 60 minutes

Objectives

- ▶ to reflect on the sustainability of our own behaviour and habits;
- ▶ to raise awareness of key issues relating to pollution and waste;
- ▶ to design a practical strategy for the group's waste disposal.

Materials

The waste cards

Preparation

- ▶ a week before you run the activity, ask participants to document all the rubbish they throw away during that week. Encourage them to record the information by, for example:
    - – taking photos;
    - – weighing their rubbish bin;
    - – counting the number of items they throw away;
    - – making a list of all items;
- ▶ make copies of the waste cards.

Instructions

Part 1: My rubbish (20 min)

1.   Ask participants to share in small groups the information they gathered about the rubbish they throw away. Give them the questions below to prompt discussion.
    - – Do you know how much (in weight) you threw away?
    - – Do you know how many items you threw away?
    - – How much food did you throw away? Why?
    - – How much packaging did you throw away?

Ask groups to prepare a brief presentation to show to the whole group.

2.   After 20 minutes, call groups together and invite them to present their results.

3.   Ask for any responses to the presentations, and use some of the questions below to debrief this part of the activity.

Debriefing (Part 1)

- ▶ Were you surprised by your own results, or those of your group?
- ▶ Do you think you threw away more or less than the average (for your country)?
- ▶ Where is "away"? Where does all the rubbish go?

Part 2: Drawing up a waste manifesto

4. Show participants either or both the quote and the videos on page 103. Then hand out the information on page 104. You could present this verbally, or make copies of the cards for them to look at.

5. Ask for comments:
    – what do you think about the information?
    – what do you find most shocking?
    – what can we – or you – do about it?

6. Take a few suggestions for the last question, then ask participants to get back into groups and draw up a list of proposals for waste in the youth centre.

    Remind them that a transformative solution to the problem of waste will address the roots of the problem: it will aim to change the rules of the game so that, for example, less plastic bottles are produced overall.

7. After 15 minutes, bring the groups back together. Ask each group to present its list of proposals. Try to make a combined list – without repetition – as they report back.

8. Check whether any of the proposals need clarification and try to reach agreement on a set of proposals from the combined list which the group wants to adopt as its manifesto.

Debriefing (Part 2)

Begin by checking that everyone is happy with the final choice – and that they feel the proposals are achievable:
  ▸ was it difficult to come up with solutions? Were any of them transformative?
  ▸ do you feel happy with the process we used to arrive at this manifesto?
  ▸ what will be most difficult about sticking to it?
  ▸ how can we support each other so that we stick to it?

Finish the session with a brief round so that each participant can speak about their reaction to the session as a whole.

Tips for facilitators

The texts and videos can provoke strong feelings in young people, so you may need to allow additional time to debrief these separately.

Participants may be tempted to focus on recycling, without thinking about the reasons for increasing amounts of consumption, and increasing amounts of waste. Encourage them to think about some of the reasons behind a culture of consumerism, and if you have time, talk about how it can be challenged – or changed.

Suggestions for follow-up

The activity "A finite planet" is a discussion activity which looks at common assumptions related to consumerism, and how these affect sustainability. "Greenwashing" looks at another aspect of consumerism: the way that companies advertise their products so that they appear to be good for the environment.

You could also try the activity "Nature journalists" with participants. This involves them collecting notes about nature – which could be in a rural park, or if you have the opportunity, by a river or coast. Depending on how close the spot is to civilisation, it is highly likely that there will be some evidence of human waste or pollution!

Ideas for action

Make sure the manifesto is put up somewhere so that everyone can see it. You could agree to meet regularly to see how well people are sticking to it, or whether it needs adapting (or improving).

Ask participants to find out whether the local council recycles waste. They could do an investigation to see how well it compares with other councils, both in the participants' own country and in some of the best practice countries. For example, participants could ask.
  ▸ Are there facilities for recycling paper, plastics, glass and metal separately?
  ▸ Are there facilities for more specialised objects such as batteries, green waste, mobile phones or other electronic equipment?
  ▸ Are all of these recycling opportunities well used? Are they easy to access?
  ▸ What happens next? Is the recycling done locally or is it shipped or transported to other countries?

Handout: Quote for Part 2:

Where's "away"?

The following is a quote from Julia Butterfly Hill, who spent two years living on a small platform on the top of a giant redwood in California, to protect the ancient forest and the tree she called "Luna".

> When you say you're going to throw something away, where's "away"?...There's no such thing. And where "away" actually is, is social justice issues and environmental justice issues. Every plastic bag, plastic cup, plastic to-go container – that is the petroleum complex in Africa, Ecuador, Colombia, Alaska, you name it. Every paper bag, paper plate, paper napkin – that is a forest. Everything that is called waste or disposable is the ways in which we are saying that it is acceptable to throw our planet and its people away. Disposables are one of the huge magnifiers of how we've lost our connection to the sacred. We just take it for granted that we're going to go to the coffee shop and get coffee that came from an exploited community somewhere where a forest was destroyed for a monoculture, put it in a paper cup that used to be a forest, put a plastic lid on top of it that used to be an indigenous community somewhere in a beautiful area, drink it, and then throw it away where it goes back and pollutes a nature community or a human community at the end.

> I am so fiercely passionate about it, because I know in my heart that as long as we are trashing the planet and trashing each other, a healthy, holistic and a healed world is not possible. We cannot have peace on the earth unless we also have peace with the earth. (Julia Butterfly Hill: *Disposability consciousness: where is "away" when we throw something away?*, www.ijhc.org/wp-content/uploads/2016/01/Hill-10-3.pdf, www.youtube.com/watch?v=72Z2wmgLiTc&feature=player_embedded#)

Handout: waste cards

Food waste

- ► roughly one third of the food produced in the world for human consumption every year, approximately 1.3 billion tonnes, is lost or wasted;
- ► every year, consumers in rich countries waste almost as much food (222 million tonnes) as the entire net food production of sub-Saharan Africa (230 million tonnes);
- ► the EU wastes about 47 million tonnes of food every year. On average, every person in the EU throws away 123 kg of edible food annually. Almost 80% (97 kg) of this waste is avoidable as it is edible food;
- ► food is wasted in all parts of the food supply chain: in farming and fishery, food manufacturing and processing, shops, restaurants, canteens and the home;
- ► in wealthy countries most of the food is thrown away by consumers who buy too much food, or by retailers who reject food supplies because of aesthetic standards: "misshapen" fruits and vegetables are not welcomed in most supermarkets.

Sources: https://bit.ly/2ogdxqh, https://bit.ly/2EKiI85

Plastic pollution

We are surrounded by plastic stuff: toothbrushes, shampoo bottles, phones, computers, food containers, water bottles, pens and highlighters; even some of our clothes are made from plastic. In addition to this, most of the stuff we buy is wrapped in plastic that is thrown away after a single use:

- ► 500 billion plastic bags are used worldwide every year;
- ► a million plastic bottles are bought around the world every minute. In 2016, more than 480 billion were sold across the world. If placed end to end, they would extend more than halfway to the sun;
- ► plastic is a nightmare for the natural environment. Depending on type, it can take as long as 500 or even 1 000 years for plastic to degrade;
- ► 90% of rubbish floating in the world's oceans is plastic. According to some estimates marine water samples contain six times more plastic than plankton. Every year 1 million seabirds and 100 000 marine mammals die from plastic pollution.

Even with all efforts at recycling, 50% of plastic waste in the EU is still put into landfill.

Sources: https://bit.ly/2tkpr5M

E-waste

E-waste includes computers, cameras, TV screens, mobile phones, fridges and other electronic equipment. The amount of e-waste has been growing, both because of technological innovation and short product life cycles – driven by constant pressure to have the newest models:

- ► Europe produces about 9.45 million tonnes of e-waste annually;
- ► more than two thirds of the metal appliances and electronic products that are thrown away in the EU are processed illegally. Many leak toxins into the environment, which can have dangerous health effects;
- ► in 2014, 41.8 million tonnes of refrigerators, televisions, washing machines, vacuum cleaners and other electrical appliances were thrown away. This was equivalent to 1.15 million heavy trucks forming a line 23 000 km long;
- ► waste that could have been recovered for recycling contained an estimated 16 500 kilotonnes of iron, 1 900 kilotonnes of copper and 300 tonnes of gold, worth US$52 billion;
- ► 9 of the 10 countries which lead in per capita production of e-waste are European. Norway is the highest, followed by Switzerland, Iceland, Denmark, the United Kingdom, the Netherlands, Sweden, France, the USA and Austria;
- ► despite there being EU legislation on the collection and recycling of e-waste (see the WEEE Directive at bit.ly/1vXdIuS), only one third of the EU's e-waste was properly recycled in 2012. About 1.3 million tonnes were illegally shipped out of the EU, mostly to Africa and Asia.

Sources: https://bit.ly/2CZRhtn, bit.ly/1JGeXyZ, bit.ly/2DjIXSW

Chapter 5
Making a difference

THE IMPORTANCE OF HOPE

Hope lies now in the millions and millions of us who say: No, no. We will not accept, we will not accept your destruction of the world and your guns and your wars…

We break away from the totality of capital death in a million different ways. We commonise. We force cracks in the system. We fight for our earth, the earth of people and other forms of life, before the capitalist system destroys it completely. We fight to open a gap between the future of capitalism, which can only be death, and the future of humanity, which can still be life. (John Holloway)

Education for sustainability can sometimes appear to be about "messages of doom". While it is of course important that young people understand the full scale of the crisis facing the planet, this message can be dispiriting and disempowering. Education for sustainability also needs to inspire young people with hope, empower them to act, and give them reason to think that it is still possible to make a difference!

This chapter is about making a difference. It is about actions or activities beyond the educational setting of the youth group, perhaps involving the wider community, but most importantly, with the purpose of leading to an improvement in sustainability – however small. This improvement might be at the individual level – for example, a personal review by each of your young people of their own environmental impact, and a resolution to make some changes; it might be at the level of the youth group – for example, starting to grow vegetables at the youth centre; or it might be at the local, national or even global level – for example, lobbying the government for changes in energy policy or campaigning against a new coal-fired or nuclear energy plant.

It is important to note that while these actions may take place outside the traditional learning environment, and while they are not normally classed as "educational", in fact taking action in this way can be one of the most rewarding and effective learning experiences for young people. Participants learn essential skills, such as co-operation, consensus building, planning and creativity; they take part in practical research, thus deepening their interest in and understanding of the issues; and they are likely to be emotionally engaged and motivated, thereby helping to clarify values and attitudes.

Your role

There is no need for any special expertise or skills to take action for sustainability. When young people feel concerned about an issue, they will want to do something, and the process of trying things out, reflecting, adapting and trying again is itself a process of learning – and a success in itself. The task for youth workers and educators is to provide support in this process, to offer information, if necessary, and to create space for young people to explore the issues and exchange ideas and views.

Start from where your group is at. Allow them to pick the issue they want to work on, according to what worries them most or where they feel they can make a difference. You could begin with one of the activities to provoke their interest and give them some ideas to work with; or you could simply engage in a brainstorm, using their existing knowledge to inform the choice they make.

Use this chapter as a source of ideas and suggestions in order to guide the group's discussions. You could also look at the list of possible actions provided in Chapter 6, "Sustainability checklist".

PICKING YOUR ISSUE

Sustainability covers a multitude of issues, many of which are covered in the activities. You should allow your group to select the issues they are most troubled by, or interested in, or where they feel they can have an impact.

In Figure 14, you will find a selection of sustainability-related issues that you could present to your group. You could also ask them to brainstorm or draw a mind map of issues that they associate with sustainability – and then add any of the following which are missing.

Figure 14. Sustainability issues

Scale and scope of an action

It is useful, when thinking about taking action, to begin by identifying its possible scale and scope. This will depend both on the group's interests and on practical considerations, such as whether there are others it can link up with, whether there are local issues or groups, and how much time and investment the group can make. We can think about taking action at a number of different levels:

- the personal level: making changes in our own lives;
- the local level: acting on local issues or with local groups;
- the global level: acting globally, perhaps in an online community, or taking on a global issue.

Making a difference in your own life

Young people could start by asking themselves: what can I do to make changes in my life that support sustainability? This is the level of personal change, and many youth work sustainability projects begin at this level. The changes can be small and participants should not feel they have to aim for perfection, or change everything at once. Even the process of reviewing habits and becoming aware of any wasteful or damaging consequences of their actions can be useful.

- You could begin with an inspirational message or a film, or invite an activist or someone who lives in a way that consciously defends the environment to speak to the group. Explore what the group and what people individually are inspired to do and support them to find actions that they can incorporate into their everyday lives. Make individual plans together, share them, and check back regularly to see how people are doing. Let others know what the group is doing!

You could also start with one of the activities as a lead-in, for example "How big is my foot?", "Chicken sandwich", "Chain reactions", or any of the others. The first activity explores some of the daily routines that damage the environment.

Examples of individual actions

- refuse to accept plastic bags and take your mug with you when buying drinks away from home;
- take an interest in where the products you consume are made and how they are made and try to use products which cause less damage to the environment;
- shop at the farmers' or local markets;
- compost your green waste: make a compost bin or take your kitchen waste to a local composting site;
- where possible, travel by train or coach instead of flying, as flying is the single most climate-harming personal action;
- start a "50-kilometre diet" to eat only local and seasonal food;
- eat less meat: meat production greatly contributes to greenhouse gases;
- think before you print and use both sides of the paper;
- make handmade presents for family and friends;
- reduce the number of new items you purchase;
- turn off the lights when they are not needed;
- turn off TVs and computers while not being used;
- take shorter showers;
- reflect on the way you speak to friends: does it promote consumerism?;
- change your life: live in an eco-village or a local sustainable community;
- look for local issues which raise concerns about sustainability.

Making a difference at local level

Incredible edible

Incredible edible groups started in 2007, with a group of like-minded individuals wanting to work together to improve their own community. They started with small herb gardens and community plots. They now grow produce and work together, provide training from field to classroom to kitchen, and support local commerce.

www.incredibleediblenetwork.org.uk

While individual actions are important, they need to be supported by systemic change if we are to tackle the serious problems related to sustainability. "Thinking global, acting local" can be a step beyond individual change, but still with manageable objectives.

You can encourage your group members not only to take action in their individual lives, but also together, in their local context. Local actions can be about raising awareness, attracting others to the cause of sustainability, getting the media to talk about a problem, and showing those in power that citizens are watching and are concerned about a problem.

Use activities such as "Climate superhero auditions", "Nature journalists" or "Our futures" to spark participants' interest and inspire them to take action at a local level.

> Examples of local actions to take with your group
>
> ▸ plant trees in your neighbourhood;
>
> ▸ start a guerrilla gardening group, create edible gardens in the city or on unused ground;
>
> ▸ volunteer at a local organisation that works for sustainability;
>
> ▸ organise spaces for discussion with other young people, e.g. in schools;
>
> ▸ organise green lifestyle study circles where you can learn together with friends about sustainable lifestyles;
>
> ▸ organise local events to raise awareness about sustainability among the population;
>
> ▸ share information about advocacy or campaigns with young people and encourage them to get involved;
>
> ▸ start using a local currency;
>
> ▸ get engaged in social movements.

Buying local

The Shopping Bag Community in Budapest is a great example of a local initiative to promote sustainability. A group of young people got in touch with local farmers and organised a system where people could buy food from local farms, to be collected from a central location. The whole system was run by a group of enthusiastic volunteers, who gave up several hours a week of their time to co-ordinate with the farmers, collect the orders, and organise the collection and distribution of vegetables, dairy and meat products, preserves, bakery items, etc.

Making a difference globally

Earth Hour

Earth Hour takes place on the last Saturday of March every year. It aims at raising environmental awareness and getting people to do small things in their daily lives that together can have a huge impact. It asks people to turn off their lights for an hour, earth's hour. Earth Hour is a highly "visible" symbolic act that millions of people can easily join in with and send their message of caring for the planet. Find out more at: www.earthhour.org

This is the level at which we try to have an impact on sustainability concerns by acting globally. Sometimes these issues may feel distant to your young people: they may find it hard to see how they are related to people in China, or rainforests in Brazil, or plastic waste islands in the Pacific Ocean.

However, it is not difficult to see the connection of most of the global issues with young people's lives – and many of the activities are designed to do this. Most of what we eat, wear and use in our everyday lives connects us to people around the world and has an environmental "footprint". Our daily habits are nearly always a step away from one or more of the most urgent environmental and social problems. As a youth worker or educator, you can encourage and support young people to see these connections and to seek out responses from them to some of these problems.

Nearly all the activities highlight the connection between our lives and global issues. For example, "The cost of fashion" looks at the social and environmental costs of the clothes we wear; "Take a step forward" looks at the impact of climate change and environmental degradation on children around the world; "Fishing game" looks at industrial fishing practices. Use these activities to alert your group to the way behaviour in their country affects people in other parts of the globe.

Examples of actions with a global dimension

> join a global campaign or groups working for a sustainability issue;
> form a local section of a global movement and get active;
> raise funds for global causes;
> distribute the results of your action via social media to friends around the world;
> research, understand, learn and share what is going on around the world;
> ask your local or national politicians to present your views at international gatherings;
> show solidarity with people who are fighting for the protection of the natural environment in other parts of the world, e.g. by signing a petition online, making information available in your language, sharing it with your networks, or joining protests or civil disobedience actions;
> join protests related to supporting sustainability. Protests can also be creative actions!

Greenpeace: inspiring change for over 50 years

Greenpeace campaigns have pushed for companies and governments to change their ways so that steps are taken to secure a green and peaceful future for all humanity. Greenpeace activists are ordinary people willing to do extraordinary things to protect the environment. As a result of their activism, companies have been forced to reconsider actions, governments have shifted position – and the environment has benefited. For example, Greenpeace's actions have led to victories in stopping coal mines, phasing out toxic chemicals, banning radioactive waste dumping at sea, and an end to commercial whaling, among many other victories.

Find out more about the victories of Greenpeace campaigns for the environment: www.greenpeace.org/ international/history/

CAMPAIGNING AND ADVOCACY

Most of the actions in the previous section can be undertaken – or at least prepared for – in a single session. A campaign can take longer, and requires persistency and often a variety of tactics. The aims may be more ambitious, and may include changes in policy or even changes at the system level. It is often useful – though not essential – to engage the support of more experienced organisations, or to begin by taking part in an existing campaign in order to build confidence and skills.

If young people are motivated to make a longer-term difference, they can very easily be engaged in such actions. For example:

> a campaign to persuade schools to ban vending machines selling products of unethical corporations;
> working with local organisations to demand that the city council provide a budget for cycle routes in the city;
> gathering evidence about air quality and using the information gathered to persuade the municipality not to build a car park close to the youth club;

- co-operating with environmental organisations to lobby for education for sustainability to be included in the formal curriculum;
- collaborating with other European youth organisations to ensure that international trade agreements support sustainability goals.

Science for Change Kosovo Movement

Kosovo[1] is one of the most polluted regions in Europe. As a response to this, in June 2014, internet.artizans, UNICEF Innovations Lab Kosovo, Transitions, and the Peer Educators Network, supported by the Transition Promotion Program of the Ministry of Foreign Affairs of the Czech Republic, teamed up to launch the first-ever citizen science initiative: Science for Change. Until April 2016, Science for Change functioned as a pilot project, building the skills of young people to monitor air quality, and running air pollution measurements in three locations across Kosovo.

In 2016, Science for Change transformed itself into a youth-led environmental movement, and it has expanded its scope of work to include non-formal environmental education, air quality monitoring, mobilisation and campaigning. The Science for Change Kosovo Movement has had a number of successes, including helping to change the public narrative on air pollution as a result of its campaign "Save your children from the invisible killer".

In 2017, the Science for Change Kosovo Movement, together with local NGO Peer Educators Network, set up the first Green School Community, at the primary school Faik Konica. One of the aims was to educate teachers, pupils and parents in how to monitor air quality in their environment.

PLANNING AN ACTION

Any action, however small, needs planning, and you should make sure that the young people are involved in this planning process from start to finish. It is an important principle of youth work that young people should be at the heart of decisions affecting them: it leads to greater ownership and responsibility.

This section introduces some practical steps to assist with planning an action for sustainability. They will help to keep your group focused and will make it more likely that it achieves its objectives.

Which problem do you want to address?

In approaching the problem you want to address:
- decide with the group which issue most concerns them, or where they feel they can most make a difference;
- brainstorm some ideas together. You could take a vote at the end, but it would be better if you could get the whole group to reach consensus on a single choice;
- the issue chosen by the group might be a global issue, such as climate change, or it might be an issue at the level of the youth group, such as how much energy is used by the youth centre. Whatever the issue, you will find it useful, once the initial choice has been made, to give the group the task of drawing a problem tree to break it down further. This will give participants a clearer understanding of the problem and help in the next stages of planning.

Where do you want to get to?

Once you decide on your issue:
- think about what the action will achieve, and what success will look like. Be realistic, and think about what you expect as a specific result of your action – not the final change you hope to obtain. For example, in a heavily polluted area, if you organise an awareness-raising event, you may be able to generate interest and concern about pollution among local people, which may then lead them to reconsider whether they should use their car on a daily basis, but you may not immediately improve the air quality;

---

1. All references to Kosovo, whether to the territory, institutions or population, in this text shall be understood in full compliance with United Nations Security Council Resolution 1244 and without prejudice to the status of Kosovo.

- possible results for the group might be things like:
  - getting 50 signatures for a petition;
  - handing out 150 stickers or information leaflets;
  - recruiting new members to the group;
  - securing a meeting with a local politician.

Who is your target audience?

Your action is likely to be a step towards making the change you want to see. It will certainly influence people, even though it may not immediately reach those who can take the final decision on your issue.

There may be more than one target audience. It is important to identify the groups or individuals that you are trying to reach, and the effect you hope your action will have on them.

For example, the group might identify one or more of the following target audiences.

Target audience	Intended effect
Local residents of this town	Sign our petition
Shoppers at the supermarket	Agree not to buy Brand X
Local newspapers	Publish our press release about the action
The Mayor	Agree to a meeting to discuss air pollution

What will you do to influence your audience?

This is where you can identify what the group will actually do. The action selected might fall into one of the following categories:

- demonstrating solutions – for example, speaking about sustainable growing methods or alternative energy sources;
- awareness raising – for example, handing out leaflets or speaking to members of the public;
- educating, running lessons or workshops, writing blogs or articles;
- lobbying, by trying to influence politicians or those in power, for example by writing letters, trying to arrange meetings or going to constituency meetings;
- protest and public actions, for example involving a demonstration, march, street theatre, occupation or die-in.

Check: how is the change expected to come about?

Before you go on to plan the action, spend a little time to make sure that the method you have chosen will serve the purpose you want it to. For example, if leaflets are supposed to persuade people to stop buying Brand X:

- where is the right place to stand, so people have time (and their hands free) to take the leaflets and maybe chat to the group?
- how can you make sure people read the text?
- how can you convey the urgency of the issue without being too pushy or making people feel bad?
- what should the design look like so that the important words stand out?
- how can you make it clear what people need to do after reading the leaflet?
- can you test out the text and design on someone outside the group?

Practical issues

Before you put your action into practice, think about the practical tasks which will need to be done before-hand, and on the day:

- make a list of all the materials you will need (and how you will source them);

- make a list of tasks such as sourcing materials, making banners, designing leaflets, raising funds, etc.;
- allocate people to each task, so that each task has at least one person responsible for making it happen;
- agree on timings;
- make sure everyone is happy with their role, and agree to check in with each other regularly.

Evaluation and debriefing

After any action, it is important to sit down together and discuss how things went. Ask the group what went well, what they think they achieved, and what could have been done better. Allow plenty of time and give participants the space to share their feelings. This will help reinforce the team spirit and can be used as a springboard for planning any future actions.

Seeds for Change is a workers' co-op of experienced campaigners and co-operators that offers support to groups that confront injustice and build alternatives. It offers training, facilitation, online resources and other support for campaigns, community groups and co-operatives. Seeds for Change has developed several guides to support organisations and groups for sustainability, including guides for direct action.

www.seedsforchange.org.uk

Chapter 6
Sustainability checklist

Youth and Environment Europe (YEE) is a platform of European youth organisations aiming to encourage young people to be involved in environmental protection. The following tools are used for supporting sustainability in the daily life of the organisation:

- ▶ a sustainability policy: guiding rules on how the network should organise the activities in the most environmental way, available at https://bit.ly/2CSgWRd;
- ▶ eco-mapping the office: a self-evaluation tool to analyse and manage the environmental performance of the organisation, involving all employees in the office;
- ▶ internal audit: a tool to review the work of the organisation (for example the work of the secretariat and the board) and monitor if the organisation follows environmental principles and sustainable policies.

This chapter is about how to be sustainable while learning about sustainability. Whether you are running a youth club, leading a local project, or organising an international youth event, this checklist will help you to keep in mind some practical steps for sustainability in youth activities.

The tips and suggestions have been divided into three different sections:

- ▶ management and working practices;
- ▶ office and youth space management;
- ▶ local and international youth gatherings, exchanges and other projects.

You can use these sections as a checklist at different stages of planning and running your projects or actions.

The sources used for this chapter were Smart CSOs (2011) and DARE Greener.

MANAGEMENT AND WORKING PRACTICES

- ▶ talk about your organisation's values. Strive to cultivate and endorse intrinsic values: values which are important in themselves, like co-operation, equality or a sense of community;
- ▶ be mindful about the learning processes inside your organisation. Do they involve everyone equally? Do people feel empowered? Do they feel safe?;
- ▶ practise consensus and democratic decision making;
- ▶ create an inspiring shared vision for your organisation about the future of society. Communicating the group's hopes for a more equal, happier, less resource-hungry world will strengthen the culture of sustainability in your organisation;
- ▶ evaluate and reflect on your group's sustainability achievements based on targets you have agreed upon;
- ▶ choose an ethical bank for your organisational account, which does not invest in ecologically or socially irresponsible businesses;
- ▶ collaborate with other organisations and groups. Be aware of existing structures or institutions which encourage competition and fragmentation. Build networks and be part of a global movement for sustainability;
- ▶ when seeking funding, particularly from private companies, check that the company or source of funds is ethically and environmentally responsible.

MANAGEMENT OF OFFICE AND YOUTH SPACE

Office stationery and materials

▶ purchase office material from socially and environmentally responsible local companies;

▶ choose pens with no plastic, use refillable or eco-friendly markers, stamps, glue, tape, etc.;

▶ choose fair-trade and organic cotton T-shirts and bags for campaigning purposes.

Setting up a youth space

▶ look for green alternatives when furnishing a youth space: use second-hand or locally made eco-sourced furniture;

▶ make your own furniture, rugs, mugs, etc. using natural or recycled materials: explore techniques with participants, organise a skills workshop, get in touch with local craftsmen or recycling groups;

▶ if you have to buy new furniture, search for products with the FSC label (Forest Stewardship Council) or equivalent certification, to indicate wood from forests with sustainable forest management;

▶ for cooking, you could build a slow cooker or outdoor wood burning oven. This will develop new skills and expertise, and save on electricity or gas;

▶ grow your own food by establishing a vegetable plot, or growing vegetables in pots around the youth centre. You can arrange to collect rainwater from the building and use it in the garden;

▶ make a compost heap and compost your kitchen waste, to be used in the garden;

▶ use water-saving toilet tanks;

▶ support smaller organisations by providing office space if you have extra space in your office: advertise it as a communal space for like-minded organisations;

▶ if you share your venue/office with other organisations, fix a day where the whole house makes a "sustainability boost", e.g. by setting up recycling bins, digging or planting the garden, or doing an audit of energy use;

▶ take part in local Earth Days and environmental days by offering your space for community programmes.

Information and technology

▶ chose a green internet provider if available, or look for a company that has an ethical policy or a record of supporting social projects;

▶ if you buy new equipment, look for a high energy efficiency rating; check that the companies you buy from are not involved in activities which damage the environment or local communities (e.g. mining);

▶ make sure that computers are always turned off if not being used (e.g. overnight);

▶ use open-source software on your computers;

▶ use Creative Commons to share your work and make it accessible;

▶ be socially and environmentally aware in online communication; promote solidarity and sustainability wherever possible.

Water use

▶ use a sink for washing dishes, rather than buying a dishwasher;

▶ use a plug for the sink while washing up;

▶ look at toilet flushing: is there an option to do a half flush?;

▶ in summer, store tap water in bottles in the fridge; avoid running the tap to get cold water.

Energy use

▶ if you have a choice of energy providers, look into those which use the largest proportion of renewable sources;

▶ use low-energy light bulbs;

▶ before using any electronic items, weigh up whether they are really needed;

- use air conditioning only when necessary;
- avoid unnecessary heating of meeting rooms or other spaces: consider putting on warmer clothes instead! Set room temperature a little lower, if possible;
- use the light economically and intelligently. There is no need to light the whole room if you only work in one corner. Use daylight instead of electric light wherever possible;
- block up any draughts and make sure the building and the rooms are properly insulated. This can save a huge amount of energy!

Waste management and recycling

- try to avoid throwing things into waste (landfill). Use reusable mugs, plates, bowls and cutlery instead of plastic ones;
- choose items with less packaging;
- reuse and mend anything you can;
- separate all the waste you can recycle, including organic waste;
- put up signs to help visitors and new staff learn the "recycling rules".

Paper use

- try not to print unless really necessary;
- for printing anything non-official, use scrap paper, and print double-sided;
- for official letters, contracts, etc. print double-sided;
- any paper which is printed on one side only should be reused as scrap or for the next time you print. You can also use single-sided letters you receive from outside sources;
- reuse envelopes by labelling over the old address;
- edit documents before printing to decrease the number of pages (cut any unnecessary text, make thinner margins, use a smaller font, etc.).

Cleaning

- use environmentally friendly products for cleaning and washing up. Look into making your own cleaning products, e.g. use vinegar, lemons or baking soda;
- if the building is cleaned through a company, try to negotiate the products they use;
- instead of using unhealthy air freshener in toilets, make a natural air freshener by mixing water with some alcohol and essential oils in an empty spray bottle;
- make sure that cleaning responsibilities are shared by everyone in the group.

MEETINGS AND GATHERINGS

Travelling and transportation

- encourage participants to reduce flights, avoid connecting flights and take long-distance coaches or trains instead;
- when budgeting for travel costs, allow for a higher price limit for train and coach travel;
- use telephone and/or video conferences instead of travelling to long-distance meetings whenever possible;
- if you are travelling with the group, use public transport, bicycles or walking for short distances;
- discourage travelling by car. Encourage car sharing if a car is the only available option;
- organise car pick-up and car share for participants if public transport is not available to the venue.

Choosing venues

- try to choose venues which have an ecological approach to energy, water and catering;
- look at transport links: will participants be able to arrive and get around using public transport?;

- support eco-villages and sustainable communities by bringing projects there;
- look for possible links to the local community, involve local people in your project, and use local resources: experts, food and services;
- make sure that all participants understand and follow the guidelines for energy, water and use of resources.

During the meeting

- agree with participants beforehand about the principles you want to guide work at the meeting. This might cover behaviour, use of resources, etc.;
- be conscious of the "cost" of your work to the environment: use flip charts economically, writing on both sides, and limit the use of projector and laptops, turning them off when not in use;
- consider having your meeting outdoors if the weather allows;
- try to ensure that the local community benefits economically, socially and environmentally both during and after the meeting;
- reduce paper use as far as possible. Instead of printing copies for everyone, put all general information up in a visible place, in large print, or point participants to electronic versions of the information;
- use paper tape and write the names of participants on it with a marker, instead of using plastic name tags;
- encourage participants to bring their own pens, writing pads and mugs.

Catering food and drinks

- provide healthy, local, seasonal food, cooked at the venue, if possible;
- source food locally: support fresh, organic, small-scale, local agriculture holdings and avoid processed, packaged food;
- provide mainly vegetarian food, with vegan options;
- as snacks, provide local, seasonal fruits, nuts or baked goods. Avoid snacks made by multinational corporations;
- choose fair-trade tea and coffee, local herbal and fruit tea, or cereal coffee;
- order food quantities carefully to avoid leftovers;
- choose tap water or locally made herbal tea and lemonade instead of bottled water or beverages;
- avoid buying food or drinks packaged in tins, cans and combined material packaging;
- for an evening out, choose a restaurant based on its social and environmental policies;
- do not use throw-away plastic cups.

Bibliography

Barley A. (2001), *Battle of the image*, New Statesman, available at www.newstatesman.com/node/153475, accessed 16 February 2018.

BBC News (2007), *Tracking the true cost of cotton*, available at http://news.bbc.co.uk/2/hi/business/6612677.stm, accessed 16 February 2018.

California Academy of Sciences, *Sustainable fishing*, available at www.calacademy.org/educators/lesson-plans/sustainable-fishing, accessed 16 February 2018.

Chapman S., McPhee P. and Proudman B. (1995), "What is experiential education?", in Warren K. (ed.), *The theory of experiential education*, Kendall/Hunt Publishing Company, Dubuque.

CorpWatch (2001), *Greenwash fact sheet*, available at www.corpwatch.org/article.php?id=242, accessed 16 February 2018.

Corporate Europe Observatory (2015), *EU emissions trading: 5 reasons to scrap the ETS*, available at https://corporateeurope.org/environment/2015/10/eu-emissions-trading-5-reasons-scrap-ets , accessed 16 February 2018.

Council of Europe (2012), "Compass: manual for human rights education with young people", Council of Europe Publishing, Strasbourg.

Economic and Social Council (2002), *General Comment No. 15: the right to water*, Committee on Economic, Social and Cultural Rights, available at www2.ohchr.org/english/issues/water/docs/CESCR_GC_15.pdf, accessed 16 February 2018.

European Commission (2011), *The EU ETS is delivering emission cuts*, available at https://ec.europa.eu/clima/sites/clima/files/docs/factsheet_ets_emissions_en.pdf, accessed 16 February 2018.

European Environment Agency (2017), *Climate change impacts in Europe*, available at www.eea.europa.eu/soer-2015/europe/climate-change-impacts-and-adaptation/climate-change-impacts-in-europe/view, accessed 16 February 2018.

FAO (2010), *Tuna: a global perspective*, available at www.fao.org/docrep/017/ap939e/ap939e.pdf, accessed 16February 2018.

Forbes G. (2015), *Not just tuna: the truth behind the world's biggest tuna company*, Greenpeace, available at www.greenpeace.org/archive-international/en/news/Blogs/makingwaves/Thai-Union-not-just-tuna/blog/54299/, accessed 16 February 2018.

García San José D. (2005), *Environmental protection and the European Convention on Human Rights*, Council of Europe Publishing, Strasbourg.

Global Footprint Network, *Earth Overshoot Day*, available at www.footprintnetwork.org/our-work/earth-overshoot-day, accessed 16 February 2018.

Global Footprint Network (2003), *The ecological cost of human development*, available at www.footprintnetwork.org/2013/09/26/ecological-cost-human-development, accessed 16 February 2018.

Global Footprint Network (2017), *National footprint accounts*, available at http://data.footprintnetwork.org, accessed 16 February 2018.

Greenpeace (2012), *The hidden secret of canned tuna*, available at www.greenpeace.org/korea/Global/korea/publications/reports/oceans/2012/sep-2012-the-hidden-secret-of-canned-tuna-eng.pdf, accessed 16 February 2018.

Greenwashing Index, *About greenwashing*, available at www.greenwashingindex.com/about-greenwashing, accessed 16 February 2018.

Holloway J. (2015), *Opening speech*, available at https://davidcharles.info/2015/01/john-holloway-opening-speech, accessed 16 February 2018.

Investopedia, *Greenwashing*, available at www.investopedia.com/terms/g/greenwashing.asp, accessed 16 February 2018.

McDowell R., Mason M. and Mendoza M. (2015), *AP investigation: are slaves catching the fish you buy?* Associated Press, available at https://apnews.com/b9e0fc7155014ba78e07f1a022d90389/ap-investigation-are-slaves-catching-fish-you-buy, accessed 16 February 2018.

National Youth Council of Ireland (2015), *The Sustainable Development Goals and youth*, available at www.youth.ie/sites/youth.ie/files/SDGs_Youth_Resource%20_Pack.pdf, accessed 16 February 2018.

Ruth Cohn Institute for TCI International, *What is TCI*, available at www.ruth-cohn-institute.org/what-is-tci.html, accessed 16 February 2018.

Sipos Y., Battisti B. and Grimm K. (2008), "Achieving transformative sustainability learning: engaging head, hands and heart", *International Journal of Sustainability in Higher Education* Vol. 9 Issue 1, pp. 68-86.

Smart CSOs (2011), *Effective change strategies for the Great Transition*, available at www.smart-csos.org/images/Documents/Smart%20CSOs%20Report%20english.pdf, accessed 16 February 2018.

Turner T. (2004), "How big is my ecological footprint?", in Grant T. and Littlejohn G. (eds), *Teaching green – The middle years*, New Society Publishers, Vancouver.

UNESCO (2014), "Roadmap for implementing the Global Action Programme on Education for Sustainable Development", available at http://unesdoc.unesco.org/images/0023/002305/230514e.pdf, accessed 16 February 2018.

UNICEF, *Heat up over climate change*, available at www.unicef.ca/sites/default/files/imce_uploads/UTILITY%20NAV/TEACHERS/DOCS/GC/Heat_up_over_climate_change.pdf, accessed 16 February 2018.

United Nations, *Declaration of the United Nations Conference on the Human Environment*, available at www.un-documents.net/unchedec.htm, accessed 16 February 2018.

United Nations (1992), "Report for the World Commission on Environment and Development: our common future", available at www.un-documents.net/our-common-future.pdf, accessed 16 February 2018.

United Nations, *Sustainable Development Goals*, available at www.un.org/sustainabledevelopment/news/communications-material, accessed 16 February 2018.

Wikipedia, *Subvertising*, available at https://en.wikipedia.org/wiki/Subvertising, accessed 16 February 2018.

Worldwide Fund for Nature, *Cotton: a water wasting crop*, available at http://wwf.panda.org/about_our_earth/about_freshwater/freshwater_problems/thirsty_crops/cotton/ , accessed 16 February 2018.

World Health Organization (2017), *Climate change and health*, available at www.who.int/mediacentre/factsheets/fs266/en, accessed 16 February 2018.

Sales agents for publications of the Council of Europe
Agents de vente des publications du Conseil de l'Europe

BELGIUM/BELGIQUE
La Librairie Européenne -
The European Bookshop
Rue de l'Orme, 1
BE-1040 BRUXELLES
Tel.: + 32 (0)2 231 04 35
Fax: + 32 (0)2 735 08 60
E-mail: info@libeurop.eu
http://www.libeurop.be

Jean De Lannoy/DL Services
c/o Michot Warehouses
Bergense steenweg 77
Chaussée de Mons
BE-1600 SINT PIETERS LEEUW
Fax: + 32 (0)2 706 52 27
E-mail: jean.de.lannoy@dl-servi.com
http://www.jean-de-lannoy.be

CANADA
Renouf Publishing Co. Ltd.
22-1010 Polytek Street
CDN-OTTAWA, ONT K1J 9J1
Tel.: + 1 613 745 2665
Fax: + 1 613 745 7660
Toll-Free Tel.: (866) 767-6766
E-mail: order.dept@renoufbooks.com
http://www.renoufbooks.com

CROATIA/CROATIE
Robert's Plus d.o.o.
Marasoviçeva 67
HR-21000 SPLIT
Tel.: + 385 21 315 800, 801, 802, 803
Fax: + 385 21 315 804
E-mail: robertsplus@robertsplus.hr

**CZECH REPUBLIC/
RÉPUBLIQUE TCHÈQUE**
Suweco CZ, s.r.o.
Klecakova 347
CZ-180 21 PRAHA 9
Tel.: + 420 2 424 59 204
Fax: + 420 2 848 21 646
E-mail: import@suweco.cz
http://www.suweco.cz

DENMARK/DANEMARK
GAD
Vimmelskaftet 32
DK-1161 KØBENHAVN K
Tel.: + 45 77 66 60 00
Fax: + 45 77 66 60 01
E-mail: reception@gad.dk
http://www.gad.dk

FINLAND/FINLANDE
Akateeminen Kirjakauppa
PO Box 128
Keskuskatu 1
FI-00100 HELSINKI
Tel.: + 358 (0)9 121 4430
Fax: + 358 (0)9 121 4242
E-mail: akatilaus@akateeminen.com
http://www.akateeminen.com

FRANCE
Please contact directly /
Merci de contacter directement
Council of Europe Publishing
Éditions du Conseil de l'Europe
F-67075 STRASBOURG Cedex
Tel.: + 33 (0)3 88 41 25 81
Fax: + 33 (0)3 88 41 39 10
E-mail: publishing@coe.int
http://book.coe.int

Librairie Kléber
1, rue des Francs-Bourgeois
F-67000 STRASBOURG
Tel.: + 33 (0)3 88 15 78 88
Fax: + 33 (0)3 88 15 78 80
E-mail: librairie-kleber@coe.int
http://www.librairie-kleber.com

NORWAY/NORVÈGE
Akademika
Postboks 84 Blindern
NO-0314 OSLO
Tel.: + 47 2 218 8100
Fax: + 47 2 218 8103
E-mail: support@akademika.no
http://www.akademika.no

POLAND/POLOGNE
Ars Polona JSC
25 Obroncow Street
PL-03-933 WARSZAWA
Tel.: + 48 (0)22 509 86 00
Fax: + 48 (0)22 509 86 10
E-mail: arspolona@arspolona.com.pl
http://www.arspolona.com.pl

PORTUGAL
Marka Lda
Rua dos Correeiros 61-3
PT-1100-162 LISBOA
Tel: 351 21 3224040
Fax: 351 21 3224044
E mail: apoio.clientes@marka.pt
www.marka.pt

**RUSSIAN FEDERATION/
FÉDÉRATION DE RUSSIE**
Ves Mir
17b, Butlerova ul. - Office 338
RU-117342 MOSCOW
Tel.: + 7 495 739 0971
Fax: + 7 495 739 0971
E-mail: orders@vesmirbooks.ru
http://www.vesmirbooks.ru

SWITZERLAND/SUISSE
Planetis Sàrl
16, chemin des Pins
CH-1273 ARZIER
Tel.: + 41 22 366 51 77
Fax: + 41 22 366 51 78
E-mail: info@planetis.ch

TAIWAN
Tycoon Information Inc.
5th Floor, No. 500, Chang-Chun Road
Taipei, Taiwan
Tel.: 886-2-8712 8886
Fax: 886-2-8712 4747, 8712 4777
E-mail: info@tycoon-info.com.tw
orders@tycoon-info.com.tw

UNITED KINGDOM/ROYAUME-UNI
The Stationery Office Ltd
PO Box 29
GB-NORWICH NR3 1GN
Tel.: + 44 (0)870 600 5522
Fax: + 44 (0)870 600 5533
E-mail: book.enquiries@tso.co.uk
http://www.tsoshop.co.uk

**UNITED STATES and CANADA/
ÉTATS-UNIS et CANADA**
Manhattan Publishing Co
670 White Plains Road
USA-10583 SCARSDALE, NY
Tel: + 1 914 472 4650
Fax: + 1 914 472 4316
E-mail: coe@manhattanpublishing.com
http://www.manhattanpublishing.com

Council of Europe Publishing/Éditions du Conseil de l'Europe
F-67075 STRASBOURG Cedex
Tel.: + 33 (0)3 88 41 25 81 – Fax: + 33 (0)3 88 41 39 10 – E-mail: publishing@coe.int – Website: http://book.coe.int